Air Travel with Children

Anna Gooz

SP

Supreme Publications
Westwood, Massachusetts

Air Travel with Children

Copyright © 2010 by Anna Gooz

All rights reserved. No part of this book may be reproduced or transmitted in any form or by any means without written permission of the author.

Publisher's Cataloging-in-Publication (Provided by Quality Books, Inc.)

    Gooz, Anna.

        Air travel with children / Anna Gooz.

        p. cm.

        LCCN 2010927625

        ISBN-13: 978-0-9845396-1-1

        ISBN-10: 0-9845396-1-1

        1. Air travel. 2. Children--Travel.   I. Title.

    G151.G66 2010   910'.2

                              QBI10-600114

Editor: Dahlia Jones
Cover and Interior design: Rick Tew / Ninja Office

For my daughter, Betu

Table of Contents

Introduction	7
Part I	9
Chapter 1: Planning your Trip	**10**
Selecting the Airline	11
Selecting your Flight	13
Buying Tickets	14
Reserving your Seat	17
Frequent Flier Miles	19
Meals on Planes	20
Travel Insurance	21
Car and Hotel Reservations	21
Chapter 2: Packing for the Trip	**22**
Baggage Limitations	23
Things to Carry	24
Document Requirements	33
Chapter 3: Preparing to Fly	**37**
Preparing the Children	37

The day before Leaving	39
Dressing	40
Online Check-in	41
The Day of the Trip	43

Chapter 4: At the Airport — 45

The Check-in Process	45
Going through Security	48
The Waiting Area	50
Airport Food	51
Boarding the Plane	51

Chapter 5: The Flight — 55

Seating Yourself	55
In the Air	57
Emergency Plan	62
Landing	64

Chapter 6: Your Destination — 67

Collecting your Baggage	67
Renting a Car	68
Staying in your Hotel Room	69

Part II — 71

Chapter 7: International Travel — 72
    Documentation — 72
    Traveling Alone with a Child — 76
    Tips to Travel Abroad — 77
    Checklist for Foreign Travel — 78

Chapter 8: Children Flying Alone — 80
    Making Reservations — 80
    Preparing the Children — 82
    At the Airport — 85
    The Destination — 87
    #1 Safety Tip for Children Flying Alone — 88

Chapter 9: Traveling with Children with Disabilities — 91
    The Law — 91
    Preparations for the Trip — 92
    At the Airport — 94
    The Flight — 97

Chapter 10: Airport Security — 99
    Getting Ready for Security — 99
    Going through Security — 102

Other Air Security Tips	104

Chapter 11: Infant Safety onboard — 106
FAA Recommendations	106
Precautions with CRSs	108
Using an Unapproved CRS	109

Chapter 12: Health and Hygiene on the Plane — 110
Preventing Colds and Other Germs	110
Travel Sickness	111
Fear of Flying	112
Dehydration	114
Using Sedatives	115
Avoiding Ear Pressure Problems	117
Jet Lag	119
Alternative Health Remedies	121
Your Medical Kit	122

Chapter 13: Entertainment onboard — 124
In-flight Entertainment	125
Airline Activity Kits	127
Toy Suggestions	128

Chapter 14: Nowhere to Go   **131**

    Avoid Getting Stuck at the Airport   131

    Make Alternative Arrangements   132

    Tracking your Bags   134

    Spending Time at the Airport   136

Appendices   **140**

    Appendix 1: List of Airlines   140

    Appendix 2: Travel Arrangement Checklist   152

    Appendix 3: Packing Checklist   154

    Appendix 4: Consent Letter   159

    Appendix 5: List of Prohibited Items   161

Resources   163

Introduction

The idea of traveling with young children is daunting for most parents – it is definitely different from traveling on your own. Children bring many changes in our life, including the way we travel. Note that I said *the way we travel changes*, not that we should not travel.

For some parents, the prospect of traveling with children on an airplane can be even more overwhelming than the prospect of car travel. Children usually do not like confined spaces and airplanes are very short on space. Restless children are cranky and hard to control. Even worse, you as a parent do not control the plane. You cannot stop and take a break when the children want to get out and stretch their legs. Before you know it, tensions run high and the entire family is in tears, vowing never to travel again. Avoiding such situations is what this book is all about.

Proper and adequate planning is the key to a comfortable trip. Plan for each part of the trip and anticipate the potential problems. You know your children best and can prepare in a way that will make the trip most comfortable for them. Be flexible with the plan. Be prepared to change it if it is not working out for the children. Pack only enough activities each day that your children can handle comfortably. Children take their cues from their parents. They learn easily. If you are prepared and relaxed – the children will be relaxed. They will have fun and you will enjoy the trip as well.

I have traveled extensively with my daughter. She is 6 years old now and I have been traveling with her since she was 6 months old. We have traveled by all the usual means of transport – bus, train, car, and plane. Air travel was initially the most challenging; it took two bungled trips to figure out the best way for us to travel together.

The purpose of this book is to help you avoid bad air travel experience. This will not only improve your vacation but also help you bring up a confident child who loves to travel. This book is a step-by-step guide to plan your upcoming trip. The guide is based on my experiences, my friends' experiences, and the extensive research I have done. Please email me your suggestions so I can add them to the book and enrich it.

Part I

Chapter 1

Planning your trip

Air travel is the most popular way to travel long distances in a short time. It can take you away from home faster than any other mode of transport. You can travel to remote corners within the country or around the world. However, it is not free of stress, especially when you decide to take your children along for the ride. This is why you should plan every detail of the trip, whether you are a seasoned traveler or a novice

You may be a little nervous, but detailed planning will prepare you for any event. Just remember that a little flexibility and patience will go a long way in making your experience a pleasant one.

Step one of the planning process is making the travel arrangements. Before you make reservations, do your research. A thorough research will enable you to get the best price and best service for your needs.

Make the arrangements carefully and thoroughly. Think about what probably will happen and what could happen. For example, it helps to be prepared with extra snacks for the kids in case flights are delayed. I mention these 'what if' scenarios not to alarm you but to tell you what you should prepare for. You know your children the best. You know the times they sleep, toys they like, and what upsets and soothes them. Consider this as you make your travel and vacation arrangements. Be practical; do not plan long hikes if your children are just learning to walk, unless you plan to carry them during the trek. Cover all your basics and make arrangements that will best meet you and your family's needs.

Making arrangements will include things like selecting an airline, choosing a flight, reserving a rental car, and reserving a hotel, if required.

Selecting the Airline

Make a shortlist of the airlines that offer service to your destination from your home city. Pay special attention to airlines that offer direct service (non-stop flights). Direct flights to your destination may be more expensive compared to flights with connections. Unless the price difference is substantial, direct flights are worth the higher price. Changing flights is a hassle, and having children in tow will make it worse. Things can quickly get complicated if your flight is delayed or you miss the connecting flight. There is also a higher probability of lost luggage with itineraries that have multiple connections. With direct flights, there are no airplanes to change and your travel time is shorter.

Do not despair if there are no direct flights or if they are too expensive – you can overcome most of the connection hurdles by good planning. Just take into account that it will take you extra time to disembark from one flight, walk through the airport terminals, and take the next flight. I usually allow for at least two hours between flights when I travel domestically and three hours with international travel. International travel requires extra time, as you have to go through immigration and security (again). Avoid flight connections with less than 45 minutes between flights. Given all the delays, there is a good chance you may miss the connection.

Check out the size of the plane offered by various airlines. The size of the airplane can also affect your travel experience. Larger planes tend to have more aisle space, less noise, and often are just a little bit more comfortable. Check out the size of the plane before booking your tickets. If there is an option, take the flight with the larger plane.

Research different airlines to find out which one offers you better services when you travel with small children. Airline Web sites are a good place to start. For example, Southwest Airline has a whole section on how to travel with children and what the airline can do for you, while other airlines have little or no information at all about traveling with children. This can also indicate how much an airline may be willing to accommodate you during your travel.

Selecting your Flight

If possible, fly at off-peak days and times. Tuesdays, Wednesdays and Thursdays are considered off-peak days. Off-peak hours would be midday to early afternoon. The number of people traveling during these days and times is smaller, which means that the plane may not be so crowded and you may be able to book a cheaper ticket. You may even be able to get an empty seat next to you for an infant's car seat or for your children to stretch their legs. Monday and Friday flights are usually packed with business travelers. So are early-morning and the evening flights.

Off-peak flights also give you time to get your children to the airport at a pace that works for your family. It will give you the time to maintain your children's morning routine. This will put them at ease. Remember, the more relaxed your children are, the easier the travel will be.

Try to see if you can get a flight time that coincides with your infant's naptime. Then you can relax through the flight while your child is sleeping. If it is going to be a long flight, try a night flight. This will give the children an opportunity to sleep and will not break their routine. This definitely holds true when you are flying coast-to-coast or trans-Atlantic.

Make sure you have plenty of time between connections, when you book your flight. Airports are huge and it can take 20-30 minutes to get from one terminal to another. On some larger airports, you may even have to take a bus or train to go from one terminal to another. You may require time to go through customs and security again. The process of changing terminals is twice as slow with children versus changing terminals alone. I would suggest allocating at least one and one-half hours for connections within US and two to three hours to make connection when traveling abroad i.e. your connection is in a foreign country. This gives you enough time to go through customs, change terminals, and go through security.

Buying Tickets

You may purchase your ticket from a travel agent, travel website, or directly from the airline. Travel agents often charge a small fee but have certain advantages. They can help you design your itinerary and the vacation, especially if you are planning to visit multiple cities. Such travel may require you to use more than one airline, and travel agents are best equipped to find you the best price and more suitable service. Another advantage is that if you are stuck in an airport due to flight cancellation or weather, the travel agent can help you find alternative flights faster that you may be able to on your own. Nowadays, travel agents are almost as competitive as the travel Web sites and will often find you fares similar to those on the Web.

Planning your Trip

Travel Web sites are a great resource for researching your trip. You can check out the possible itineraries and prices, and plan your trip. The travel Web sites often offer the lowest fares and have the facility to book the entire vacation. You can make hotel and car reservations as well.

You should also check out the airline's Website to see the prices and special offers that the airline might have. The airline Web sites often carry great last minute deals. They may also offer a discount on children's tickets. If you book your tickets online, there are no booking fees. However, if you call customer service to make a reservation, you may be charged up to $50 per ticket depending on the airline.

Tip	Use your credit card!
	Buy your ticket on your credit card. You can get value points on your credit card. Some credit cards also offer free travel insurance, if you use the card to buy the tickets.
	Remember to pay the card at the end of the month so that you do not have to pay any interest.

Airlines do not require you to pay for children under the age of two. Infants and children under the age of two, traveling within the United States, Canada, Puerto Rico, and the U.S. Virgin Islands may be held on an adult's lap during the flight at no additional charge. However, FAA recommends that you buy a ticket for the infant and that the infant should travel in a seat that has been approved for use in an airplane. FAA calls these seats a child restraining system or CRS. I discuss the requirements for a child restraining system in a later section. Only one un-ticketed infant can travel with one adult. If you have twins and you are traveling by yourself, you will have to buy the ticket for at least one infant and the other one can travel as an un-ticketed infant.

If you do want to buy a seat for your child, some airlines offer special discounts for children under the age of two,. These discounts are usually not available from travel Web sites, so you have to contact the airline directly to get these special prices. Airlines can ask for documented proof of age for any traveler including children. Please be prepared to provide the appropriate documentation, such as birth certificate, passport, etc., upon request.

I recommend reserving a seat for a child under the age two, unless it creates a serious financial burden for you. The child is much safer in a seat than on your lap in case of an emergency landing or if your flight runs into some turbulence in the air. If you are traveling alone or are traveling at peak times, the additional seat will make the travel much more comfortable for you and your child. You and the infant will have more space and yours hands will be free. The infant will be able to sleep comfortably during the flight and you may get a chance to catch-up on a book from your ever-growing reading list.

Airlines do not allow you to carry a car seat in the plane unless you have paid for a seat for the infant.

The overhead luggage bins do not have enough space to store a car seat. If you want to take a chance with finding an empty seat next to you, bring the car seat and a large plastic bag that can be used to cover the car seat. If there are no empty seats on the plane, you can always pack the car seat in the plastic bag and check it as luggage at the gate before boarding.

Children, two years old and over, must travel in a purchased seat. Most airlines offer a 20% to 40% discount on tickets for children and these discounts are usually available only from the airline's own Web site or through customer service.

Warning	Read the fine print on your ticket!
	These days airlines charge for small items that in the past we as travelers used to take for granted. You may be charged for baggage, favorable seat assignment, and even headphones and blankets. Sandwiches and meal boxes are often available for purchase on the plane. Carry enough cash, based on your anticipated needs.

Reserving your Seats

Reserve your seat assignment when booking your ticket. If you cannot get the seats assigned at that time, access your booking on the airline's Web site as early as possible. Most airlines allow you to access your booking online to make changes. You can reserve your seats by making changes to the booking. You may also call the airline's customer service to reserve your seat.

Do not leave the seat assignment to the last minute. Make sure your seats are together and try to get a window or an aisle seat. Chances are the middle seat next to you may be empty. This will give you some space and make traveling a little bit easier, especially if you did not buy bring an extra seat for the infant.

There are seating restrictions when you travel with children. For example, Children (or adults with children) under the age of 15 (12 years for some airlines) may not be seated in a seat next to an exit. Reserving seats early ensures that you will get the best seats. Seating restrictions vary by airlines – check with your airline.

You can also ask for the bulkhead seat - especially if flying on international flights.. These seats usually have more foot space than the regular seats in the plane. They are usually reserved for people traveling with infants or people with special needs. Ask for these seats in advance although not all airlines allow you to reserve them. Sometimes you may have to get to the airport a little early if you want to get these seats. If you are traveling abroad and you are traveling with infant, these seats are a must-have. The airline provides you with a bassinet for the infant to sleep in. These bassinets can only be used with bulkhead seats. This frees up your hands and you can relax. The infant can also sleep lot more comfortably.

Some discount airlines do not assign seats before the check-in. Passengers are seated on a first-come, first-serve basis. You have to pay to get seat assignments in advance on these airlines. Recently, some other airlines have also started charging travelers a fee to reserve the "desired" seats. These seats have some extra legroom or may be towards the front of the plane. However, in most cases, you will not be required to pay additional fees. If you want to reserve your seats anyway, find out about the plane that the airline plans to use for your flight. This will give you the information on the layout of the plane and help you pick the best seats. You can also check out Web sites like seatguru.com and seatexpert.com. These Web sites have seat-plan drawings of coach cabins for different airplanes. After all if you going to pay, you should know what you are getting.

Frequent Flier Miles

Enroll your child in the airlines frequent flyer program. You may already be enrolled in the frequent flyer program yourself but it may not have occurred to you to enroll your child too. Often children get full points even with child fare seats. If you are paying for the seat, you might as well take advantage of the miles (both for yourself and for your child). The simple act of signing up can earn your child thousands of miles toward a free trip with many airlines.

Even if you think you are traveling only this one time, you may want to register your children for the frequent flier miles. In some airlines, you retain the miles you acquired for your lifetime, and in other cases you can keep the miles for a few years before they expire. After the success of this trip, you never know how frequently you may be flying. You could also donate these miles to a charity if you do not use them again.

Meals on Planes

Most flights within the continental US do not offer meals anymore. However, they are still available on a most long distance flights, especially if you are traveling on to a foreign destination. It is a good idea to ask your airline if any meals will be served onboard. If your flight has meal options, book your and your kid's meal when making your reservation. There are special meals available for children – ask for them. Remember - if you want to order special meal, they have to be ordered 48 hours before the flight.

You can make a special meal request by calling the airline's customer service or by updating your booking online on the airline's Web site.

Travel Insurance

When you are traveling with children, life is even more unpredictable than it normally is. It is a good idea, before you begin your trip, to get adequate travel insurance to cover ticket and even hotel costs. This will cover you in case you are unable to travel or have to change plans. Sudden illness like the flu, ear infections, etc. might call for a change of travel plans. I have had to change plans when my daughter came down with the flu and we had to extend our vacation by two days. Travel insurance came very handy then to cover the additional costs we incurred. In addition to these costs, travel insurance also covers baggage lost or destroyed during travel. It does not cover normal wear and tear of baggage.

Car and Hotel Reservations

If you need a rental car at your destination or need to stay in a hotel, reserve them. You can do this online on full service travel Web sites like Orbitz.com or Travelocity.com. Alternatively, you could call individual hotels or rental car companies.

You can request a car seat or a booster seat from the car rental company if you do not plan to carry your own. You can also ask the hotel for a crib in the room if you require one. These services may carry an additional cost but will ensure your and children's comfort and safety.

Chapter 2

Packing for the Trip

Once your tickets are reserved, you may be worried about what to carry with you and what to leave behind. You feel like you should carry as much as possible so that the children 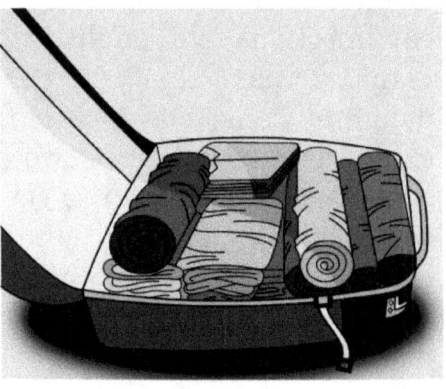 are comfortable. You also know that you have limited space and that you may have to pay extra for excess baggage.

Children are very adaptable and can often survive and actually enjoy themselves without a lot of the modern accessories we think they need. Pack according to your children's needs and only the essentials. Travel as light as possible. Remember – you will have to carry what you pack. It might sound like a hard thing to do with children but it is not impossible. And believe me after the trip, you will realize that you had still packed too much.

Make a list of all the things you would like to carry before you start packing. Then divide the list into three parts: 'must haves', 'should haves' and 'would like to have'. Now you really know what you actually need and what you want. You are ready to start packing.

Baggage Limitations

Airlines restrict the amount of baggage you can take with you. Some airlines offer lower fares but allow less baggage. Some airlines do not allow a full baggage allowance for child fares. You would have to pay for any excess baggage you carry over the allowed limit. These fees can be as high as $50 per bag. Call the airline or check their Web site to find the baggage restrictions that apply to you before you start packing. Check the size, weight, and number of bags you and your family are allowed to take on the airplane. Check the information for carry-on luggage as well as the check-in baggage.

Carry-on and checked baggage allowances for children vary depending on whether or not a seat is purchased for the child. On most airlines, if an infant sits in your lap, you are not allotted space for the infant's bags. However, if a seat is purchased, the standard carry-on and checked baggage limits apply on most airlines. The following items are allowed over and above the carry-on allowance for a traveler with an infant:

✓ Approved child safety seat for the child (if there is an empty seat available, otherwise it can be folded to fit under the seat in front of you)

- ✓ Umbrella stroller

- ✓ Diaper bag

These items are allowed even if a seat for the infant has not been purchased.

Things to Carry

Check-in Baggage

Check-in baggage should contain all the items you will need during your trip but not during your flight. You cannot access these bags once you have checked-in with the airline for the flight. Check-in baggage tips are as following:

- ✓ Check-in baggage should be within the allowable baggage limits set by the airline or you will have to pay excess baggage fees.

- ✓ Checked-in baggage sometimes gets misplaced or lost. When packing, mix items for each member in all the bags. This way even if you are left with only one bag temporarily, at least everyone will have something to wear.

- ✓ Keep extra plastic bags for dirty laundry, shoes, etc.

- ✓ Toddlers need twice as many clothes as babies or older children.

- ✓ Pack a copy of your itinerary and other travel documents for back up. Keep a photocopy of your passport for a backup.

- ✓ Do not pack any money or original copies of important documents.

- ✓ If your phone has data access and it will work at your destination, you can use it as your telephone, contact list, map, etc. Just remember to carry the charger with you.

- ✓ Try to leave some space in one of the bags, and leave it open, so you can put any last minute items or snacks in it.

Items for your Check-in Bags

Here is a list of things you may be packing. Treat this list as a starting point and add or remove items to suit your family needs.

- ✓ Clothes: The amount of clothing will depend on the length of your trip and the opportunities you will have to wash your clothes. One-piece outfits and loose-fitting clothes are often easier and quicker to pack, as you do not have to spend time matching the pieces. Think of all the activities you may be doing or attending, and pack accordingly. Remember to pack plenty of undergarments.

- ✓ Clothes for special occasions: If you are going to attend a wedding, graduation, or special occasion, make sure that you pack all the necessary clothes. Keep an extra set for children to cover any unforeseen event.

- ✓ Shoes: comfortable walking shoes and other shoes, boots, sandals, etc. as needed for your trip.

- ✓ Toiletries: toothbrush, toothpaste, dental floss, comb, baby soap, shampoo, shaving kit, moisturizer, safety pins, Ziploc bags (plenty of these), cotton balls, nail clippers.

- ✓ Accessories: The list of accessories may depend on the area you are going to and the time of year. In general, the list may include socks, hats, mittens, sunglasses, scarves, and rain gear like an umbrella and raincoats.

- ✓ Coats, jackets, and sweaters: if you are traveling in winter or are going for a holiday in a cold place, you will need things to keep you warm.

- ✓ Bathing suits and life jacket (if needed): if you are planning a beach holiday, remember to carry your bathing suits. Pack a life jacket or floatation device, especially if your children are young and just learning to swim.

- ✓ First aid kit with thermometer, band-aid, vitamins, and drugs like acetaminophen/ibuprofen, and your prescription medicines if you take any – Keep a letter from the physician in the first-aid kit and in your carry-on bags regarding the need and the use of the prescription medicines. Customs officials often scrutinize the medication and may limit the quantity.

- ✓ Camera, camcorder and related accessories such as batteries, chargers, and blank CDs or DVDs for recording

- ✓ Cell phone with charger – Most cell phone and laptop chargers work at both 120 volts and 220 volts. You may have to carry an adapter to make sure that your charge fits in the electric outlet at your travel destination.

- ✓ Infant related items: diapers or pull-ups, diaper rash cream, wet wipes, bibs, pacifiers, bottles, sippy cup, clothes, socks, and shoes.

- ✓ Toys: drawing paper, crayons, stuffed animals, books, portable CD or DVD player with CDs or DVDs. Take only the ones that your children really like; if your children do not like stuffed toys, they will not start playing with them just because they are on vacation.

- ✓ Plastic and zip-lock bags: I carry plenty of these and use them to throw away stuff, store dirty laundry, and keep food and toiletries organized.

- ✓ Car seat: Car seats may be used on the plane, if they are approved by the federal aviation authority (FAA), and at your destination in the car. Car rental companies do not always supply a car seat, even if you ask for one when making the reservations, and often charge extra for it.

- ✓ Breast feeding equipment if you use it.

- ✓ Travel guides and maps: I use my Blackberry phone to access this information and have stopped carrying actual maps.

- ✓ Swiss army knife with a bottle opener, pen knife, etc. – I carry this to open the plastic ties that are used to secure the zippers of my checked-in bags. I keep it in the outside pocket of the checked-in bag. Remember: you are not allowed to carry any sharp objects in your carry-on bag.

- ✓ Special items to childproof your hotel room like electric outlet covers, cable ties, night light etc.

Tip	Use distinctive, fun tags!
	Tag all bags with distinctive tags so that you can identify your bags from a distance. Many bags look alike and you can easily pickup a wrong bag at the baggage claim. These tags will help you identify your bags from a distance. Fill in the baggage tags with your name and contact information.

Carry-on Baggage

Concentrate on your carry-on baggage once your check-in bags are almost ready. Remember you are going to have to manage all this baggage along with your children for the entire trip. Keep the carry-on baggage to a minimum and your hands free of clutter so that you can handle the bags and the children at the same time. Simple tips for managing your carry-on baggage are:

- ✓ Use a backpack for your carry-on bag as it will leave your hands free. A backpack with wheels can be wheeled around the airport, but is heavier than regular backpacks.

- ✓ Leave the diaper bag at home. Pack all diaper bag items in the backpack as well.

- ✓ Pack your backpack in the reverse order of things that you may use. For example, anything that is for emergency only, like an extra set of clothes for you, place at the bottom of the bag. Keep diapers in a handy spot at the top of the bag.

- ✓ Keep your travel documents handy. Put them in a fanny pack or a bag that can be tied to your waist or in a pocket of your backpack.

- ✓ Empty your wallet of unnecessary cards, receipts, and coins.

- ✓ Label your expensive items like portable CD/DVD player and cell phone with your contact information. If you leave them behind somewhere, like on the airplane, the finder would know how to get in touch with you.

- ✓ If your children are old enough, let them carry their own backpacks. Let them also pack the bag – it will increase their sense of adventure and ownership. Keep these bags light; remember you will be carrying these as well when the children get tired.

✓ If you are traveling with an infant, bring plenty of formula pre-made for the flight. It can be hard to prepare the drink on the airplane. If your infant prefers warm bottles of formula, carry a thermos of boiling water and add some to the bottle. On larger planes, the attendant can usually warm the bottle for you. Remember to test the temperature of the bottle before giving it to your infant.

✓ If the infant only eats baby or pureed food, bring your own food. Prepackaged jars work well, as they can be eaten cold and they do not spoil in the original packaging.

Tip	**Use disposable everything!**
	Use disposable items as much as possible while traveling. You get use disposable diapers, wipes, bibs, changing pads, etc. Get baby food packed in prepackaged containers or disposable food containers. Get disposable plastic cups and spoons to feed the toddlers. You can discard the use items as your trip proceeds and your carry-on bag will get lighter. You will also not have to lug around dirty items around and when you arrive at your destination, no cleanup is required.

Items for your Carry-on Bags

Here is the list of items you may want to include in your carry-on baggage:

- ✓ Important documents (see the document section below).

- ✓ Food: Take easy-to-pack foods like fruit, granola bars, fruit bars, crackers, raisins, and nuts. Take fruits that do not leave a mess behind for you and the airline crew to clean up. Grapes are a better choice than bananas or oranges. While deciding on quantities take into account potential flight delays and some extra traveling, i.e. pack some extra food. Many countries have strict quarantine laws and you are not allowed to bring fresh fruits, plants, or raw seeds into the country. If you traveling abroad, check the quarantine laws before you bring any such food items. Even if you bring such item, consume them on the airplane or dispose them before you get off the airplane at your destination. If you are traveling within USA, this does not apply.

- ✓ Drinks: Drinking is important. Take at least one bottle of water per person, more if using infant formula. Juice boxes are also easy to carry. With increased security at the airports, you may have to buy the water and juice after you go through the airport security. You are only allowed to carry small amounts of liquids through the security checkpoints.

- ✓ Carry some gum or soft chewy candy like gummy bears etc., as these can be very helpful for relieving ear pressure during take-off and landing. They also help distract the children.

- ✓ Carry an extra set of clothes for the infant and at least one t-shirt for yourself. Accidents happen and you want to be prepared.

- ✓ Toiletries you may use during traveling, like a comb and moisturizing cream. Do not bring more than you will require on the airplane, you can pack everything else in the checked-in bags. Carry some instant hand-sanitizer to keep yourself hand germ free.

- ✓ Plenty of diapers and wipes - use disposable diapers on the trip. They are a lot more convenient and safer (less chances of leaks) than cloth diapers during travel.

- ✓ Disposable baby items like changing pads, bibs, paper tissue – You can always bring regular changing pads and bibs. I love disposable items as my hand bag becomes lighter as the travel proceeds and I am not carry a pile of dirty items.

- ✓ Infant blanket/sheet: You will need this to wrap your infant. It can get cold on the plane and if the infant falls asleep, this can help him or her stay warm. On longer flights, you can get blankets on the airplane; grab a couple as soon as you get on, as they tend to go fast. I often rely on these blankets as that is one less thing for me to carry, and if my daughter creates a mess on it, someone else will take care of it. I just place it in one of the extra plastic bags I carry and leave it on the seat. However, if your child has allergies or is very sensitive, bring a blanket from home. Note that many airlines have started eliminating blankets from their coach class or have started charging for the blankets. Do bring one from home – if there are blankets on the plane, you do not have to use your own. If you are breastfeeding, the blanket should be large enough to cover you and the child during feeding.

- ✓ Toys for the flight: Some toys that work well on airplanes are a favorite soft toy or blanket for comfort, 2-3 crayons with a coloring book or an activity book, small plastic toys such as cars (no wheels), dolls or animals, erasable slates with an attached pen, and CD or DVD players for older children

- ✓ A car seat for infants or umbrella stroller for toddlers: You can use the car seat in the airplane if you have an empty seat next to you. The umbrella stroller can be used to move around at the airport and at the destination. These items can be gate-checked if required.

Document Requirements

Traveling within the U.S.

Travelers under the age of 18 are not required to present a photo ID for domestic U.S. travel. Identification from the accompanying adult is accepted. However, in the current security climate, you may be asked to present proof of age (such as a birth certificate) at the airport for any children under the age of 18 who are traveling with you. It is good idea to carry a copy of the birth certificate and a school ID, if available.

You, and anyone else over the age of 18 in your party, need to have government-issued photo identification for traveling within the United States. Some examples of valid forms of ID are:

✓ Current state-issued photo driver's license OR

✓ Current state-issued photo identification card OR

✓ Current passport OR

✓ Employee ID issued by a Federal, State or local government agency

Traveling outside the U.S.

All passengers who are traveling outside the United States are subject to the same travel document requirements. This means you and your children will need to have valid passports and visas where applicable. Visit the U.S. State Department's Web site for information on passports as well as visa and immunization requirements for international travel.

Medical Records

Take along a copy of your child's pertinent medical information and their pediatrician's phone numbers. When traveling overseas, ask your doctor or health service for a pediatrician referral.

If your child is on medication, be sure you have enough for the entire trip. Keep only the required portion of the medication, plus some extra for backup, in the carry-on bag with a copy of the prescription. Pack the rest of the medicine in the checked-in baggage with another copy of the prescription. Keep the prescribing physician and pharmacy's contact information handy, just in case.

Other Documents to Carry

Apart from the valid photo ID, here are other documents you should consider carrying:

- ✓ Cash or ATM/check card: I do not like to carry a checkbook. In any case, most vendors do not accept out-of-state or international checks.

- ✓ Credit and Debit cards: Carry only 1-2 credit cards. Do not carry department store type credit cards because they are not going to be required on the trip and just add to the bulk in your wallet. In addition, if your wallet is lost or stolen, you have to deal with only one or two card companies.

- ✓ Pictures of the children: I rarely carry hard copies of these as I have the pictures on my camera and cell phone.

- ✓ Health insurance card or other relevant documents: you should carry only the medical insurance card, and leave the dental and other insurance cards at home.

- ✓ Airplane tickets or a printout of your e-tickets
- ✓ Travel insurance documents
- ✓ Rental car reservation information
- ✓ Hotel reservation information
- ✓ Printout of your itinerary, important phone numbers and addresses: Keep a copy in each piece of packed luggage. Leave a copy of your itinerary with at least a couple of family members or friends.
- ✓ Club Membership cards like AAA are useful for getting discounts at hotels, theme parks, etc.
- ✓ Vaccination documents, if required
- ✓ Addresses and driving directions to get around when you reach your destination

Chapter 3

Preparing to Fly

Tickets have been booked, packing is almost complete, and you are ready to go. However, your children may not be ready yet. You have to prepare them for the plane ride and get ready to enjoy the trip. You also have to make arrangements that everything at home runs smoothly when you are away.

Preparing the Children

You may have prior experience with flying and may feel comfortable with the idea of flying. However, for your kids, it's a different story; this is their first airplane ride. They may share your excitement, but may also be scared a little. If this is their first trip away from home, they would be even more nervous.

You must help them get comfortable with the idea of going away and traveling on an airplane. Build upon their sense of excitement and ease their fears. Some common tips and techniques to prepare the children are as following:

- ✓ Discuss the overall trip. Tell them why you are all taking this trip and how you expect the children to enjoy themselves. If they are going meet family, show them pictures of the family members they are going to meet.

- ✓ Talk about the airplane ride well in advance of the trip. Tell them about the travel plans and get them involved in each step. Let them choose their own outfits to pack and select toys they want to carry on the airplane.

- ✓ Explain to them what to expect at the airport and during the flight. You could describe to them the airport procedures such as the check-in process and the security checks. Tell them about the engine noise, ear pressure, turbulence, and other things they may be experiencing during the flight.

- ✓ Visit the airport before the actual trip.

- ✓ For reading time, choose books with airplanes and traveling themes.

- ✓ With older children, you can visit various Web sites for children that provide information on flying and airplanes.

If you fear flying yourself, do not show it in front of the children. If they see or sense that you are scared, they may also develop a fear of flying. This first flying experience will build the foundation for future trips for your children. You want this trip to go as smoothly as possible.

The Day before Leaving

The day of travel is very close. You are about to leave for the big trip tomorrow. You should finalize all the travel arrangements and do the following to get a perfect start for your travel day:

- ✓ Reconfirm all your reservations. You may be required to reconfirm 48 hours in advance for international flights.

- ✓ Lay out clothes and shoes for everybody for the next day.

- ✓ Check your bags to make sure everything is packed and ready. Lock all bags except one, where you can add any last minute items. Make a list of last minute items you may need to pack and put this list beside the bags so that you will remember it.

- ✓ Put labels on all the bags with your name, destination address, and contact number.

- ✓ Walk around with your carry-on luggage and make sure you can carry it comfortably.

- ✓ Make a document with your complete itinerary, hotel and car reservation information, and other relevant information. This document consolidates all your travel information and makes it easily accessible.

✓ Make labels with your name and contact information. Put these labels inside the children's pockets. I hope that you will not need to use them but they can give you a sense of security. Give some cash to the older children. It can be useful if they are separated from you at the airport.

✓ Arrange for transport to the airport. Plan for extra time just in case your cab is stuck in traffic, your car has flat tire, or your friend is late picking you up.

Dressing

I usually dress more for comfort than for fashion. This is especially true when I travel. Remember, though, that it gets cold in the airplane after a while. A fancy tank top may be fine at the airport, but you will freeze in it on the airplane. Simple tips for dressing for travel are:

✓ Wear loose and comfortable clothes.

✓ Dress in layers. You add a layer if it is too cold or remove a layer if a spill happens.

✓ Dress the children in layers too.

✓ Keep an extra t-shirt or two for yourself in your hand luggage.

- ✓ Keep some toiletries like a comb and a moisturizer (and a lipstick for women). These will help you look neat and feel better.

- ✓ Dress in clothes without metal buttons or zippers that may trip off security alarms as you go through the metal detectors.

- ✓ Eliminate large metal jewelry pieces.

- ✓ Dress the children in bright colors so you can spot them easily around the airport. You could also color coordinate the whole family.

If you are breastfeeding, dress in appropriate discrete nursing clothes. There is no privacy on the plane. Proper dress will help you feel more at ease. Taking a large blanket along will also help you keep your modesty.

Keep three to four extra sets of clothes for babies and toddlers, and at least one set of clothes for the older children. Accidents and spills happen. This is the first trip for the children and they may not react well to air travel.

Online Check-in

Most airlines now allow you to check-in from any computer even before you leave home. You may be allowed to check-in up to 24 hours before your flight is scheduled to leave. The online check-in process is usually fast and easy. It can save you hours at the airport and make travel a little easier. With on-line check-in you do not have to get to the airport early and stand in a long line to check-in. The online check-in process works as follows:

- ✓ Go to the airline Web site from any computer
- ✓ Start the check-in process by entering the ticket or reservation number
- ✓ Confirm the itinerary and details of the travelers
- ✓ Enter the number of bags that you want to checked-in
- ✓ Select the seat
- ✓ Print the boarding passes or email them to yourself

You are done with check-in. Once you get to the airport, you can drop your luggage at a designated spot, go through security, and proceed to the boarding gate. It is as easy as that.

You may not be able to check-in online if you are traveling to or from a foreign country or if your party is more than ten people. If you have special requests on your ticket, like a wheelchair assistance request, child under 14 traveling alone, etc., you also may not be able to check-in online. These requests require some action on the part of the airline agent at the airport, so present yourself to the agent for check-in.

Once you have checked-in, it is not easy to change your flight. You may have to pay extra to make any flight changes. These changes can be done only prior to the departure of the flight. If you miss your flight for any reason, you are in trouble. You may have to buy brand new tickets at full price to travel.

Check your airline's Web site to find out about their online check-in process and its rules and restrictions.

The Day of Trip

Finally, the big day is here. You are nervous, but ready. Wish yourself 'good luck' and remember to keep your cool and your children relaxed. Here are the last minute items to do:

- ✓ Start the day just as you would any other day (if possible). Try to stick to your daily routine as much as possible. This will help everyone stay relaxed.

- ✓ Remember the list you made yesterday of last minute items to pack? Pack them now and lock all the bags.

- ✓ Confirm that your transport to the airport will be available on time. Remind your friend or family member to pick you up on time, or re-check the taxi or airport bus service.

- ✓ Check the weather and call the airlines to make sure your flight is on time before you leave the house.

✓ Shut off all unnecessary appliances and electronics. Do not turn-off the freezer if you have food in there.

Finally it is time to leave. Turn off the lights, turn on your security alarm, lock the doors, and off you go. Enjoy your trip.

Chapter 4
At the Airport

Get to the airport well in advance and be prepared. It takes longer to get through the  airport with children. Another advantage when arriving early is that the check-in counters are largely empty and you will get done with the check-in process quickly. Most people get to the airport close to flying time and then spend considerable time standing in line. It is a lot easier to control the children in an airport lounge while having some snacks than in the check-in line. I try to get to the airport about 1½ hours before a domestic flight and 3 hours before an international one.

The Check-in Process

If you have already checked online, you can skip this step. But you still have to hand over your check-in baggage and get a baggage receipt. Here are some tips for a smooth check-in process, if you are planning to check-in at the airport:

- ✓ Give yourself plenty of time for the check-in process, especially if you are traveling during holidays or if you have a lot of luggage

- ✓ Ensure you get the best seats. If you are traveling with an un-ticketed infant, ask if the flight is full. If the flight is not full, the agent can allocate you a seat next to an empty seat. Some may even block the seat next to you.

- ✓ If you check-in your car seat, ask the agent to put it into the big plastic bags that are available at the airport, usually for no charge. Without it, your car seat may get dirty and smelly by the time you get it back. I recommend you carry a large garbage bag big enough to cover the car seat. You can use it store the car seat, if you check it in.

- ✓ If the flight offers meals, find out if the meal you had booked is available. If the meal has not been booked, you cannot request at it this time. This means you may not have anything suitable to eat for you or your children, especially if you have any dietary restriction. If you did not get the requested meal, buy appropriate food items from the airport after you go through security.

- ✓ Make sure the frequent flyer information is available for each traveling member of your family on the travel reservation. If it is missing, you can add the information now. You cannot enroll in the frequent flyer program at this time if you or the children have not enrolled before. You can keep the boarding pass and enroll later, usually within 6 month of the travel, to get the frequent flyer miles.

- ✓ Keep the boarding passes and the baggage claim stubs in a safe place. You may be required to show the baggage stubs before you can take your bags out of the airport at your destination.

- ✓ Put the airline identification tag on each piece of carry-on baggage. Do fill it out with at least your name and a telephone number. This will enable the finder of the bag to contact you in case you leave it behind.

- ✓ If you are traveling alone with an infant and the first class or business class check-in counter is empty, go ahead. You will find that other passengers and the airline staff will give you some leeway if you are traveling alone with children.

- ✓ Last, but not least, remember to smile sweetly and helplessly when your children throw a tantrum in the middle of the line. Maybe someone will let you jump the queue.

Using a Self-Service Kiosk for Check in

Airlines encourage you to use self-service kiosks these days. Here you can check-in, get your seat allocation, generate stubs for your checked-in bags, and get your boarding passes. This can help you avoid long lines at the check-in counter. Using kiosks is a good idea when:

- ✓ Everyone who is traveling with you is booked under the same itinerary. Otherwise, you will have to repeat the check in procedure for each person and may have a hard time getting seats together.

- ✓ You already have your seat allocation. The booth gives you an option to change your seats, but you will probably find that most seats are full by this time.

Once you have checked in, remember to hand your bags over to the attendant. The attendant will put the label on the bags and give you the stubs. Read the stubs to make sure that the correct label was put on the bag and it will get to your destination with you.

Going through Security

Everyone must go through security screening to go into the departure area. Even babies must be individually screened. However, you will not be asked to do anything that will separate you from your child.

Security staff is usually trained at handling children going through security, but it is a good idea to talk to the children about the process before they go through security. This will make them more comfortable. Speak to your children again about the

At the Airport

screening process so that they will not be frightened or surprised. Remind them not to joke about threats such as bombs or explosives.

The screening process has two main parts:

✓ X-Ray

- All carry-on baggage, including children's bags, stroller, and car seat must go through the X-ray machine. You will need to fold the stroller or slings so that they can go through the x-ray machine.

- When equipment does not fit through the X-ray machine, it will be visually and physically inspected. Ask screeners for assistance with your bags and equipment, if needed.

- Remember! Do not leave the infant in the carrier or the seat while it goes through the X-ray machine.

✓ The walk-through metal detector

- Before walking through the metal detector, empty your pockets and all your children's pockets. Place your and kid's shoes in the bins provided. This way you can minimize the chances that the alarm will go off. If the alarm goes off, the screener will need to resolve the cause and this takes longer than removing and putting on shoes.

- If child can walk, let him or her walk on its own through the detector. Otherwise, you can carry the child.

- You cannot take the child through the metal detector on the stroller or the carrier. However, if your child has a disability, security staff will not remove the child from the equipment without your permission.

With ever-growing security threats to airports and air travel, airport security has introduced tougher regulations. There is long list of do and don'ts, and if you follow these, you will avoid delays and hassles. Please see the chapter on airport security for detailed security-related information.

The Waiting Area

Locate the gate from which your flight will be taking off after you get through security. Go to the gate and make sure everything is in order. If you get there more than an hour before the flight is ready to board, the gate area may be empty. Airline staff will open the counter at the gate about half an hour before the boarding time.

Now you can relax a little. Settle down at a spot that will give you a good view of the airport. As you wait for the flight, keep the children busy. This can tire them out and they may be quieter on the airplane. Supervise them, but let them move around the gate area. Let them peek out of the windows and look at the airplane activity outside. Do not let children out of your sight at anytime.

Airport Food

This is a good time to have a snack. Depending on how your children take to flying, you may not get any time on the plane to eat or even drink. Airport food is usually not healthy and is pricey. It is a good idea to bring a healthy snack from home if you can. If you plan to buy food at the airport, there is usually plenty of choice at larger airports. Small airports usually have a coffee shop or two.

Do not eat heavy and fried food before the flight. Such foods can make the children queasy during take-off. Stick with light food, and small portions. If they fill up on food, they are more likely to be queasy.

Make sure everybody has a drink of water or juice. Fill up your bottle and children's sippy cups with water for the plane and make sure you have plenty of water for the infant. If not, buy a bottle of spring water. Do not use water from water fountain for very young children.

Boarding the Plane

The airplane crew starts the boarding process about 30-45 minutes before take-off. Change your infant's diapers before boarding starts. There is always more space to change diapers in the restrooms at the airport than in the airplane. This way you can avoid changing diapers on the airplane if the flight is three hours or less. Take the older children for a restroom break as well before you board the plane.

Gate-check any items that will not be allowed in the airplane cabin, like strollers, a car seat if you have been unable to obtain an extra seat on the plane, or large carry bags. The airline agent may ask you to gate-check large carry bags if the flight is completely full. Remember that any item that is gate checked is not accessible to you during the flight. Take out any items you will need, before you gate-check any bags.

Airlines offer travelers with young children the option to pre-board. This allows you to board the airplane before everyone else and gives you a few extra minutes to settle in. I used to pre-board when my daughter was just an infant. It gave me time to set up her car seat, that was approved for the airplane use as well, and make her comfortable in it. As she became a toddler, I found that pre-boarding did not work for us. It was just more time for her to be cooped-up in a tiny space. She would be restless even before the plane was ready to take off.

Remember, even though airline provides you the option, you do not have to pre-board. You can let the children move around and play in the gate area until all the other passengers are onboard. This way, when you board, it is almost time to take off. By the time you and the children settle down, the airplane doors are closed and the plane is ready to go.

The airplane's air conditioning system is turned off during the boarding process. The airplane can get very warm and uncomfortable. If you pre-board, the children can easily get warm and would be fidgety. The air conditioners are turned on after the doors close. The flight attendants also tend to be more helpful if you board in the end. After all, they are in a hurry to get you seated. They are anxious to get going and make sure the plane leaves on time.

If you are traveling with another adult, one of you should board early with the carry-on baggage. The other person should stay at the gate with the children and board at the end. The person, who boards early, will be able to find space in the overhead bins to store the baggage. He or she can also take out the items that would be required during the flight and put them in the seat pockets at the front of your or the children's seats. It is very hard to find space in the overhead bins ever since airlines have started charging for checking-in bags. Travelers pack all they can in their extra-large handbags.

If you are flying with a low cost carrier that does not assign seats, you should board early. Often the airplanes are full and people tend to take window or aisle seats first and leave the center seat empty. If you board at the end, you may find and your children are sitting separately. In that situation, I have found that most likely someone would volunteer their seat, rather than sit with someone else's child, but why take the chance?

Gate-check your stroller as you board. You will get a receipt from the attendant. Once you get to your destination you will get the stroller back at the gate when you leave the plane.

Chapter 5

The Flight

By this time, you will surely be feeling a lot more confident. You were able to prepare for the trip, get the children to the airport, check-in for the flight, go through security, and board the flight  without an incident. You may have butterflies in your stomach from worrying about the flight, but relax – this may now be the easiest part. It will be over and done with before you realize it.

Seating Yourself

Settle the children first. Put their seat belt on. Give them a toy or a sippy cup to keep them occupied. If are going to use a car seat for the infant, place the car seat on the airplane seat and secure it with the seat belt. Then put the infant in the car seat. The car seat should face the rear of the plane for babies under 6 months of age and face forward for older babies.

Do not seat the children in the aisle seat. They enjoy reaching out and exploring and can bump their arms into a person or a serving cart passing down the aisle. You can seat the child in the window seat and sit next to her or him. This will minimize the chances that your child will disturb other passengers seated in your row or get hurt by bumping into something. If you are traveling with another adult, seat the child in the middle seat between you.

Unpack your handbag and take out only the things that you will definitely need, for example; plastic bags, napkins, wet wipes, a couple of toys, food etc. This places important items you need within your reach without having to go through your bag every fifteen minutes. Keep the bag with the items you may need during the flight under the seat in front of you and the bag that does not require to be opened during the flight in the overhead bin.

Once the children are settled, you can settle down yourself. Look around and try to warm up to the fellow passengers around you. Do not get discouraged by 'Oh my God! Children!?!' look you may get. Smile sweetly and appear confident. This will assure your fellow passengers that you are in control and can control your children. You could even try some witty icebreakers. Most people get over it, and if they don't, then tough luck! You already have your hands full – do not worry about them. Just be polite and go about your business.

Once the doors of the airplane are closed and you can hear the engine revving up, prepare for take-off.

Offer baby a pacifier or a bottle. Give the children some gummy candy to suck-on. This will help equalize ear pressure and minimize discomfort or pain. Ask the children to sit back. Give them a toy to divert their attention. If you are traveling with an infant on your lap, make sure the infant is comfortable. If you have a car seat that has not been approved by FAA for use in an airplane, you will have to hold the infant in your lap during take-off (and landing).

As soon as you can get the attention of a flight attendant, ask him or her for a children's entertainment kit offered by the airline. If the attendants have any entertainment kits onboard, they will get one for each child either after everyone is seated or after the flight has taken off. You will rarely get a kit on a domestic flight, but it is usually available on long-distance and international flights. This kit is a brand new toy for the children to explore and will keep them occupied for a little while.

In the Air

Here are some common pointers you can follow on the plane to make the flight more pleasant.

- ✓ Avoid dehydration: The air circulating in the plane is very dry and can cause babies and young children to become dehydrated. Encourage children to drink often during the flight. This may result in an extra bathroom trip but is better than getting dehydrated. If you are a breastfeeding your child, you are also in danger of getting dehydrated and should take a few sips of water regularly. See chapter 10 for more information on dehydration

- ✓ When the flight attendant offers drinks, always accept, even if you or the children may not drink it immediately – the flight attendant may not be back to serve it later. Save the unopened juice can for later in the flight. You can pour the drink in your children's sippy cup for later. On long flights, if food is not going to be served, bring something to eat for the children and yourself or carry cash to buy sandwiches offered for sale on the airplane.

- ✓ Babies have difficulty adjusting to changes in their schedule. Try to maintain the infant's regular feeding and sleeping schedule as much as possible. If this is their normal naptime, try to settle them down for a nap, even on the plane.

- ✓ Keep children entertained with whatever toys you may have brought. You are responsible for your children at all times during the flight. Do not let them out of your sight, even for a minute. They can wander into dangerous areas such as the galley. Seat them away from the aisle so that they have to go over you to go into the aisle. Take your nap while they are napping. Do not let them run in the aisles and definitely do not let them kick the seat in front. If you take your children around the plane, hold their hands and

✓ do not let them touch other passengers' belongings.

✓ If the children are crying loudly, make a visible effort to comfort them. Other passengers do not appreciate crying children, but are more supportive if they see you are at least making an effort.

✓ Apologize to other travelers for any inappropriate behavior from your children. You do not have to apologize if they cry or are uncomfortable. However, if they kick the seat in front or accidentally hit the passenger in the adjoining seat, ask the children to stop immediately and apologize to the affected passenger.

Infant's Bottles

Milk for babies and children is usually available on board the plane if you ask for it, but the flight attendants can run out of it, so carry some powdered milk as a backup. If your children drink formula, get enough pre-made formula to last the duration of the flight and some extra powder as a backup.

You can also ask the attendant to warm the bottle for you. Check the temperature of the liquid yourself before giving it to the children. Do not rely on the attendant, as she may not know how warm your children like their drink.

Restroom Use

Airplane restrooms are compact and challenging even for adults. They are even tougher for young children as they do not have any special seat covers that the children may be using at home. Here are some tips to help you tackle the toilet issue:

✓ Take the children to use the restroom before the flight attendants serve drinks or food. There is usually a longer line after the service. If there is a line, guide the children through the line.

✓ Accompany your children to the restroom on the plane. Point out the location of the toilet paper, the hand soap etc. The airplane toilets make a very loud noise when flushed. Flush the toilet once in front of the children so that they are prepared. Ask them if they are comfortable using it on their own. If they are OK, let them go in on their own and wait outside until they are done. Do not let them lock the door as it may be confusing for them to unlock it. If they are not comfortable on their own, you should get into the restroom along with them. It is a tight fit, but do close the door to give your children some privacy.

✓ There is usually a line for the toilet, especially on long flights. The line can be long after meals. You should try to take the children to the toilet before the meal is served or half an hour after the meal trays have been removed.

✓ If your children are newly toilet trained, consider using diapers during the flight. Accidents do happen, as you may well be aware.

Diaper Changing

Changing diapers on the plane may be unavoidable when you are traveling with babies. Prepare a "diaper bag" in one of the plastic bags you have with you, as you settle in your seat and the airplane takes off. Put just one diaper, a few wipes, and lotion or rash cream (if you use any) in it. Keep it in the seat pocket ready for use. I suggest using disposable diapers – you can dispose a dirty diaper and do not have to carry the smelly bundles of clothes with you.

You may change the baby's diapers in the airplane restroom. The airplane restrooms may or may not be equipped with a changing table. If there is a changing table, most likely it will be small and accommodate only infants. When you take your seat, find out from the flight attendant if there is a restroom with a changing table suitable for your children on the airplane. Remember that the restroom with the changing table may not be the one closest to your seat location and prepare accordingly.

If there are no changing tables on the airplane, you will have to change the diaper on your lap. This works only with small babies, who can actually fit in your lap. It is a good idea to practice changing diapers on your lap before you come onboard. After all, you do not know if your flight will have changing tables.

There are other options. If you have the bulkhead seat, you can spread out the changing pad on the floor and change the diaper. You can also change diapers on the airplane seat itself. Cover the seat with a changing pad, and go ahead and change the diaper. I would do this only as a last option when there was no other passenger in the adjoining seat. You have to be quick if you decide to change a diaper in the main cabin. Dispose of the diaper in the closest restroom and wash your hands – do not give the dirty diaper to the attendant.

Once you are done changing and return to your seat, prepare your "plastic diaper bag" for the next trip. Use the instant hand-sanitizer and hand lotion with you for good hygiene.

Emergency Plan

Statistically, airplanes are the safest mode of transportation. However, it is important to prepare for emergencies. This will help you keep your children safe under all circumstances.

Preparing for an Emergency

Pay attention to the standard pre-flight emergency information. Take note of the nearest emergency exits and familiarize yourself with the location of the flotation devices. Ask the flight attendant if there are special flotation devices for small children and babies onboard.

If your child has a medical condition, like asthma, that may become an issue during the flight, let the flight attendant know before the flight, and carry your child's medication with you.

Evacuation Plan

Have an evacuation plan during the trip. If you are traveling alone with one child, it is quite straightforward: you will grab your child and proceed to the nearest exit. Have a plan to exit the airplane if you are traveling alone with two or more children. You may have to ask the flight attendant's help to evacuate. If you are traveling with a partner, you both need to know who is responsible for which child during an emergency.

If your children can walk, talk to them beforehand. Let them know that they have to follow the flight attendant's instructions and your instructions in case of any emergency.

You will probably never have to put your evacuation plan into action, but it never hurts to have one in place.

Precautions you need to know about

If oxygen masks are deployed in the airplane, put your mask on first. This ensures that you will not pass out and can help you children throughout the emergency. Remember, you cannot help the children or yourself, if you are incapacitated.

Keep the children in their seats with the seat belts on as much as possible. Turbulence can happen at any time and if the children are not secure at that time, they may get hurt. If you have to take the children out of their seats, do so only when the seat belt sign is turned off.

Landing

When the plane gets ready for landing, settle the children back in their seat and secure their seat belts. Give them something to suck on, or to drink, just as you did during take-off. If the flight is during the day, encourage them look out the window. "Sightseeing" can distract them and keep them in their seats during landing. You should secure your own seat belt as well.

Take all your belongings before exiting the airplane. Check under the seat and in the pockets of the seat in front of you. Collect all the garbage in the plastic bag that you brought with you – the flight attendants will really appreciate that.

It is best to wait for the other passengers to get off the airplane first – you do not want the children to get hurt as people rush to exit the airplane. This will also give you enough time to collect all your belongings. Encourage the children to collect their own items. This will distract them and they will not be jumping to get off the plane. If you are traveling with another adult, one of you could get off the plane with the children first, while the other person can collect all the items and get off later.

> **Tip**
>
> **OOPS! Forgot _____ on the airplane**
>
> It happens. The children are crying, you cannot wait to get off the airplane and you forget something either under the seat or in the back pocket of the seat in front of you. It can be hard to get your belongings back but not impossible.
>
> Here is what you should do:
>
> ✓ If you remember the items immediately after getting off the airplane, you can go back and get them.
> ✓ If you have left the gate but are still in the airport, go back to the gate. If the plane is still at the gate, you could request the gate attendant to get the item for you from the airplane.
> ✓ If you cannot go back to the gate, file a form at the airlines baggage desk located near the baggage claim area.
> ✓ If you have left the airport, try to go back to the airport and check at the baggage desk if your lost item has been found.
> ✓ If you cannot go back to the airport, call the airline baggage desk at the airport.
> ✓ Finally, you can call the airline or file a 'lost item form' online.
>
> You have a higher probability of finding your belongings if you act as soon as you know

> that your belongings may be missing and you have left them on the plane.

At the gate area, collect any items that you have gate-checked like the car seat, the stroller, or the extra bag that you could not take into the plane cabin with you. Sometimes you may have to wait for a few minutes at the gate area to get your belongings. Proceed to the baggage claim area once you have collected your gate-checked items.

Congratulations! You have almost made it. You have reached your destination and the butterflies in your stomach should be settling. You might have a headache but you have a good reason to celebrate: you have successfully completed your first flight with your child.

Chapter 6

Your Destination

Congratulations! You are now officially on vacation. You have reached your destination and are still in control. There are a few more steps to complete 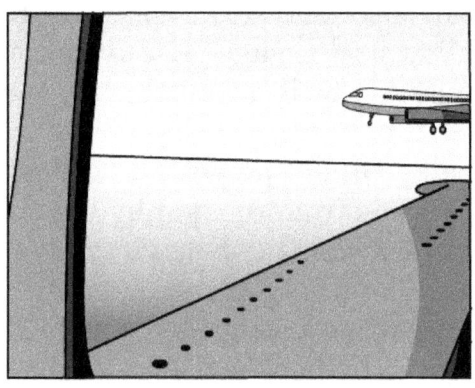 and then you will be well on your way to enjoying yourself.

Collecting your Baggage

After getting off the plane, you still need to collect your checked-in baggage. Follow the signs to the baggage claim area. Children are full of built-up energy when they get off the plane and are aching to stretch their legs. Let them walk around, but do not let them get out of control. Hold their hands and lead them on to the baggage collection area.

In the baggage claim area, do not let children run around the conveyer belt area. It can be dangerous as people are pushing around heavy carts and can hit your children. Do not let the children run on the conveyer belts either. Their foot or clothing can get entangled in the moving parts of the conveyer belt. This obviously can be very dangerous.

Do not let small children push or play with the cart. Older ones can push it under your supervision and can have some fun doing so. Remember to pick up all your baggage. If any piece of your baggage is missing, wait for all the baggage from your flight to be unloaded. Check around the baggage conveyer belt. Other passenger may have removed your baggage from the belt by mistake and may have left it next to the belt. If you still cannot find the missing bag, you can file a Missing Baggage form at the airline's baggage counter. They should be able to tell you where you missing bag is and when it will arrive. Usually the airline will deliver the missing bag to your hotel, or wherever you may be staying, free of charge.

Renting a Car

You can rent a car from any rental car company's airport check-in counter. If you have made an advance reservation, your car should be ready for pickup when you check in. You may want to inquire with a couple of rental companies if you do not have a reservation.

At most large airports, you may have to take a shuttle to the office of the car rental company to pick up the car. If you are traveling with another adult, one of you should stay at the airport terminal while the other one goes to get the car. Children are more easily entertained in the large open area of a terminal than in the confined space of a shuttle bus.

You may need a car seat or a booster seat for the children. If you haven't brought your own car seat, you will have to rent one from the rental car company. Make sure that the car seat you get is the correct size for your child's height and weight. If you will be traveling a lot by car, try to get a minivan or a car with a DVD player to keep the children entertained.

If someone is picking you up at the airport, remind them to arrange for a car seat ahead of time, if you are not going to bring your own.

Staying in your Hotel Room

Finally, as you check-in at your hotel and heave a big sigh of relief, there is just one more task left. Your hotel room is not childproof in all likelihood. Here are some things you can do to ensure the safety of your children:

- ✓ Check the location of the exits and fire extinguishers on your floor.

- ✓ Try to get a room on the first floor, as balconies can be very dangerous. The railings are quite wide and small children could go through them. If that is not possible, you would either need to keep the balcony door locked at all times or get some netting and attach it outside.

- ✓ Tie up electrical cords and window blinds with rubber bands.
- ✓ Cover electrical outlets.
- ✓ Move small items found in a hotel room like water glasses, soaps, lotions, pens etc. out of reach.
- ✓ Keep the bathroom door closed.
- ✓ If the hotel has provided you with a crib, check it to make sure it is safe and working properly.
- ✓ Use a night light for the children.

Do not plan any activities for the rest of the day. If there is still daylight outside, take the children for a walk. This will help you all recover from jet lag. Have a light dinner and make it an early night. You are at your destination and your vacation has just started successfully.

Part II

Chapter 7

International Travel

Traveling to a foreign country places some additional responsibilities on you. You have to meet documentation requirements to enter a foreign country and to return home. Depending on your destination, you will need to take extra precautions and may need to pack more items.

Documentation

Everyone in your traveling party, that is, you and the children, require appropriate travel documentation. The two most important travel documents are your passport and your visa.

Passports

A passport is the best documentation with which to prove your US citizenship and identity. Some countries accept a birth certificate as proof of identity and citizenship, especially when accompanied with a state-issued identification like a driver's license.

A valid US passport is required to re-enter the country by air since the 9/11 attacks. This applies to children as well. Note that documentation requirements are different for travelers crossing the border by either sea or land. In that case, the documentation requirements depend on where you are traveling from and the age of the children.

Ideally, you should obtain all passports, including those for the children, before you make your reservations. All children must have their own passport. Adding a child's name on the parent's passport is no longer an option, as it was in the past.

The passports should be valid for at least 6 months after the date of your trip, otherwise, you will need to renew your passport. Check with the nearest consulate of the country that you plan to visit for their requirements regarding passport validity dates.

Passports will be checked at the airline check-in counters. You will not be allowed to board the flight if you cannot show proper documents for you and your children.

Visas

Not all foreign countries require you to have a visa. Most countries in North America, like Canada, Mexico, various Caribbean countries, etc., and Europe do not require US citizens to obtain a visa. If you are a permanent US resident, you will be able to travel to most countries in North America with your permanent resident card and the passport from your home country. In any case, check with the nearest consulate of the country that you plan to travel for specific visa requirements and related fees.

Obtaining a visa can take time. It pays to plan in advance and get all visas at least a month in advance of the trip. Check the visa as soon as you get it to make sure all details and dates are in order.

The U.S. State Department, Bureau of Consular Affairs' Foreign Entry Requirements web page is http://travel.state.gov. This site includes the entry requirements of foreign countries and the addresses and telephone numbers of foreign embassies and consulates in the United States. You should confirm any information you find directly with the embassy or consulate of the country you are planning to visit as it may change any time.

Pre-Travel Vaccinations

Apart from the standard childhood vaccinations, you might need to get your children additional vaccination depending on where you are going. Here are some vaccinations that you should check with your doctor:

- ✓ Influenza vaccine may be needed to reduce the risk of influenza infection during the high-risk season, or in areas where there is a 'flu epidemic'. For example, in US the most common season for flu is November-February.

- ✓ Hepatitis A vaccine may protect infants and children from the Hepatitis A virus (HAV), which is common in many parts of the world. People traveling to remote regions of Mexico and Central America are routinely advised to get this vaccination.

- ✓ Yellow Fever vaccine protects against the disease of the same name that is transmitted by mosquitoes. It is common in some areas of Africa and South America. Under World Health Organization rules, some countries can require a proof of yellow fever vaccination. Check with the consulate of the country that you plan to travel to.

- ✓ Typhoid vaccine can help to prevent typhoid fever that is an acute, life-threatening febrile illness caused by the Salmonella bacteria. Note that this vaccine is not fully protective and you will have to make sure that food and water are not contaminated.

- ✓ Meningococcal vaccine helps to prevent Meningitis. This disease can be fatal, especially for children. Meningitis epidemics are recurrent in sub-Saharan Africa during the dry season and Centers for Disease Control recommends travelers should be vaccinated before traveling to this region in this season. Saudi Arabia requires visitors to be vaccinated during the annual Hajj.

- ✓ Japanese Encephalitis is spread by night-biting mosquitoes in rural areas of Asia and the Pacific Rim. You may be at risk if you are planning to spend a lot of time outdoors or are going to stay for an extended period in the rural areas. Vaccination is available to prevent Japanese Encephalitis.

- ✓ Malaria is another disease you need to talk to you doctor about. It is common in tropical regions of the world and is spread by mosquitoes. There is an oral medication to prevent malaria.

Before traveling, you should talk to your doctor and discuss what you can do, apart from vaccination, to prevent these illnesses. You should also find out about symptoms of the diseases that may be relevant in your case. This will help you identify the disease at the earliest opportunity and seek medical help.

AIDS/HIV TESTING: Some countries have regulations regarding AIDS testing, especially for long-term visitors. Check with the Consulate of the country that you plan to visit to verify if this is a requirement.

Traveling Alone with a Child

If you are traveling with children alone, you may be required to show proof that the absentee parent has given permission for your children to travel with you. You should carry a signed and notarized document of permission from the absentee parent. There is a sample letter/form in Appendix 4 that you can use.

You should also carry the children's birth certificate to show that you are the actual parent. If you have the sole custody of the children, you should carry the relevant documents as proof. If you are traveling with somebody else's children, carry a notarized letter signed by both parents.

Tips for Traveling Abroad

You can take the following additional steps to ensure you and the children have a safe and pleasant trip when traveling abroad:

✓ Register with the state department before you leave the country. This enables the State Department to contact you in case of an emergency or a crisis, and assist you. You can register online at https://travelregistration.state.gov

✓ Review all your documents for validity and completeness. Sign the passport and the visa (if required). Fill out the emergency information page on the passport. Complete this information on the children's documents as well.

- ✓ Leave copies of itinerary with family or friends. They can contact the State Department who will contact you in case of an emergency.

- ✓ Check your overseas medical insurance coverage. Call your insurance company and find out if emergency medical care will be covered during your trip. If you do not have the required insurance, consider buying some.

- ✓ Carry contact information for the local US consulate in the country you are visiting. You can contact the consulate for assistance during your trip

- ✓ Learn about the laws and customs of the country you are visiting. Find out about the current law and order situation there. This will help you prepare for your trip appropriately.

Checklist for Foreign Travel

Checklist to follow before traveling to a foreign country:

- ✓ Make sure all passports are valid.

- ✓ Obtain visas if required.

International Travel

- ✓ Take care of medical and dental checkups for yourself and the children. Make sure all needed vaccinations are up to date.

- ✓ Get proof of required vaccinations or AIDS test if needed.

- ✓ Get documentation for the children if you are traveling without the other parent.

- ✓ Get travel insurance to cover any emergencies abroad. Make sure that the coverage is appropriate.

- ✓ Check with the U.S. State Department for any travel advisories for the country you are traveling.

- ✓ Get a good guidebook and get to know your destination. Find out about local laws and customs.

- ✓ Make copies of your passport, insurance policy, emergency numbers, and travel details. Leave these copies with family/friends.

- ✓ Take enough money for the trip. Find out what you will be allowed to bring back with you before you go.

Chapter 8

Children Flying Alone

There may be a situation where you are forced to send your children alone on an airplane. This can be very  worrying for parents and children alike. However, you can minimize the risks and make the trip comfortable for the children if you plan well.

Many airlines, including all of the major U.S. airlines, allow children as young as five to travel alone. In addition to the usual risks that come with flying, there are additional risks that are associated with children flying alone. Many of these risks can be overcome by using common sense and taking a few basic precautions. The following information will help the parents and/or caretakers make the best possible arrangements for the children traveling on their own.

Making Reservations

Airlines allow children over the age of five to travel alone. However, you know your children and what they can cope with best. Talk to your children before you make any travel arrangements. Children must show confidence that they will be able to tackle the challenge of traveling alone, even though they might be a little scared. It is always helpful if they have traveled on an airplane before. If not, you can still prepare them so they can take the journey with confidence.

You can go ahead with the reservation once the children are ready to travel. Make reservations that are most suitable to your children's needs.

Select an Airline

Before making any reservations, inquire about the Airline's policies about children traveling alone. Almost all airlines will let children aged from 5 to 15 years to travel alone as an unaccompanied minor. Actual individual ages may vary, and you should check with the airline of your choice.

Find out what paperwork and identification will be required for your child to travel as an unaccompanied minor and what other restrictions may apply. You should also ask questions as to how the airline will ensure the safety of your child; how they ensure that the children will make the connections, etc. Compare as many airlines as you can and pick one that suit you best.

Select the Flight

If possible, select a nonstop flight. Flights with stopovers and connections increase the possibility of complications during the children's trip. Some airlines allow unaccompanied minors only on nonstop flights.

Try to get a mid-morning flight. The airports are less busy when you take your child to the airport and, if the flight is delayed, the children will reach their destination in good time. Avoid the flights later in the day or in the evening. A delay can cause the children to be stuck at the airport at night on their own, especially if they have to take a connecting flight. Many airlines do not allow unaccompanied minors on the last flight of the day.

I recommend that you buy the ticket for an unaccompanied minor directly from the airline. Then you will get accurate information to all your queries. When making reservations for a minor child, identify the child to the airline reservations agent as an 'Unaccompanied Minor' and provide the child's age. Be sure to notify the airline of any special issues about your child, such as medical conditions.

If the children have to change airplanes, you must arrange for them to be escorted between gates. Airlines charge you extra for this service, but it is required for children under the age of 12 and is recommended for older children. Older children can change terminals without assistance but may not be able to deal with potential problems.

Preparing the Children

Talk to your children. Explain to them why they have to go on this trip on their own. Tell them who will meet them once they reach their destination. Assure the children that they are completely safe. Read books to them on traveling, do role-plays and any other activity that will make them more comfortable with the idea. You should also explain the whole flight process to them. Tell them about:

✓ Boarding the airplane: Explain the boarding the process to the children. Tell them that you will wait with them at the gate but will not be able to board the airplane with them. The flight attendant will help them get on the plane before the other passengers. You will not be able to come in the airplane with them, but you would be outside until the plane leaves the gate.

✓ Asking for help: Let them know that they can ask the flight attendant for any help on the plane. At the airport, they can approach the airline agent directly without standing in line. Tell the children that they must keep the 'unaccompanied minor' badge around their neck at all times. This helps the airline staff identifies them promptly and provide assistance.

✓ The precautions to take: Explain to the children about all the safety precautions they must take. They should not talk to strangers. They need to pay attention to flight attendants and follow their instructions. The children also need to keep their seat belts fastened during the flight. If they require help at the airport, or are separated from the airline assigned, they should only approach a uniformed airline person or the airport police. They must never leave the airport alone or with a stranger.

- ✓ Discuss suitable behavior with your child: Take the time to discuss proper behavior with your children. Tell them that they should be polite to everyone around them and should not disturb other passengers either by talking loudly or by playing in the airplane aisle. They must inform the flight attendant if any other passenger shows inappropriate behavior, such as talking rudely, threatening, touching inappropriately, etc.

- ✓ Changing planes: If your children are going to change planes to get to their final destination, explain the process. Usually, the airline assigns an agent who will take the children from the arrival gate to the departure gate of the next flight. If possible, avoid an itinerary where the children have to make a connection.

- ✓ Contacting you in an emergency: Tell the children how to contact you, if required. If they carry a cell phone, they can always call you. Alternatively, you can take them to a pay phone at the airport and show them how to use it either by using coins or by making a collect call.

Packing for the Trip

Try and pack as much as you can in the check-in baggage. The children should carry the minimum possible carry-on baggage. It is hard enough for children to take care of themselves and it is helpful if they do not have to lug around a large bag with them. The following items must be included in the carry-on bag:

- ✓ The actual paper ticket, or the e-ticket printout and the complete itinerary

- ✓ Identification documents and any other paperwork required to travel

- ✓ A notebook with contact names, phone numbers, and addresses at home and at their destination, including information of the person who will be picking the children up at the destination

- ✓ Enough cash to buy snacks at the airport and to make a telephone call

- ✓ Cell phone, or instructions on how to call you

- ✓ Entertainment for the plane like books, activity books, DVD player with DVDs, etc.

At the Airport

Plan to arrive at the airport with extra time on hand. Remember, you cannot check-in unaccompanied minors online or at the service kiosks.

Check-in

When checking in your children for their flight, identify them to the airline check-in agent as an "unaccompanied minor". You have to complete the "Unaccompanied Minor" form, which requires contact information about the parent/guardian at the origin and at the destination, and alternate contacts. You can also download this form online from the airline's website and fill it before you come to the airport. The check-in agent will give you a badge for the children traveling. The badge has a pocket that will usually contain a part of the unaccompanied minor form. The children must wear this badge for the entire travel. It helps the airline employees identify the children as unaccompanied minors.

You will receive the boarding pass for the child and an "escort pass" for yourself after you complete the check-in process. The "escort pass" enables you to go through the security checkpoint and accompany the children to the gate. If you have check-in baggage, the baggage claim tickets and baggage tags should match your children's final destination. Place the claim ticket in the notebook or the packet with rest of the documentation.

Departure Gate

Identify your children to the gate attendant as unaccompanied minors when you arrive at the flight departure gate. Your children will be allowed to pre-board the flight. If you arrive at the gate after the flight has begun boarding, the children will be allowed to board after all other passengers have boarded. The children are introduced to the flight attendant as unaccompanied minors as soon as they board the airplane. Some airlines require you to wait at the departure gate until the flight takes off.

The Destination

You should find out as much as possible about the destination airport before your child leaves home. You can go to websites like http://www.airportterminalmaps.com and http://www.airlineandairportlinks.com to get information such as airport terminal layouts, features, and amenities, flight information etc. This information will help you prepare the children and tell them what to expect at the arrival airport.

Your children are released only to the person(s) specified on the unaccompanied minor form at the destination. The person taking custody of the children can get an escort pass from the check-in counter to pass through security and come to the flight's arrival gate. He or she must show proper identification to take custody of the children. It is not enough that the children recognize the person(s) who has come to take custody.

Take all possible steps to ensure that your child is met by either the primary person or the alternate person as specified in the Unaccompanied Minor form. The airline can return the children to the origin at your expense, if no one meets the children and you cannot be contacted.

> **Tip**
>
> **#1 Safety Tip for Children Flying Alone**
>
> Coordinate! Coordinate! Coordinate!
>
> Coordinate every detail with the person who is responsible for picking up your child from the airport. The person's name should be spelled out exactly as it appears on the government issued photo ID that he or she plans to use when taking custody of the children. He or she must have all the details of the children's itinerary and know when the flight is expected to arrive at the destination. He or she should know if bags have been checked-in on behalf of the children.
>
> Call and let the person know once the flight has departed and confirm the expected arrival time. The person should get to the airport at least half an hour early. Sometimes flights do arrive early! He must bring the photo-ID as previously determined.
>
> Keep in constant touch with the person. If, for any reason, you cannot contact the person you have identified as the primary contact to take custody of the children, contact the alternate person you selected on the unaccompanied minor form immediately, so they can pick up the children from the airport.

Your children may also be turned over to the local police or social services if no one comes to take custody of the child and you cannot be reached.

Checklist for Children Flying Alone

✓ Inform the reservations agent that a child will be traveling alone, and the child's age.

✓ If possible, make a reservation on a nonstop flight that departs mid-morning or thereabouts.

✓ Take a trip to the airport prior to the actual flight to familiarize the child with the airport. This is especially important if the child has not flown before.

✓ Keep a copy of child's complete itinerary, including flight numbers, flight schedule, baggage claim information, etc.

✓ Coordinate with the person meeting the child at the destination. He or she should have exactly the same information as you have, and must provide a valid photo ID to the airline representative releasing the child.

✓ Arrive early at the airport to allow ample time for check-in and security process.

✓ Fill out the unaccompanied minor form completely. Do not leave any portion blank.

- ✓ Introduce the child to the gate attendant as an unaccompanied minor. Let the attendant know if the child has never flown before or if the child requires any special attention.

- ✓ The child should be carrying an ID, some cash, and items for entertainment during the flight.

- ✓ You should remain in the gate area until the child's flight has departed, if possible.

- ✓ Remind the child not to talk to strangers or leave the airport with anyone.

Chapter 9

Traveling with Children with Disabilities

Traveling with children with disabilities is challenging but can be a rewarding experience. You have to take a few extra precautions to make sure that your child will be safe and comfortable during the trip. Precautions and preparations will vary based on the type and severity of the disability of the child.

Note: This chapter uses "child" instead of "children". The use of "she" does not denote any gender bias and is used as an abbreviation of "he or she".

The Law

There are national and international laws to protect the rights of disabled air travelers, including disabled children. The US federal government enacted the Air Carrier Access Act (ACAA) in 1986. The ACAA is designed to eliminate barriers and discrimination faced by disabled passengers. It has provisions regarding airport and airline accessibility, seating on the airplane, and services and equipment that must be provided by the airline. All airlines must make available a copy of the ACAA to any traveler upon request. The International Civil Aviation Organization issued a circular with guidance to all international airlines about the accommodations that should be provided to air travelers with disabilities.

Preparations for the Trip

Contact the airline and find out what services are available for your child depending on her disability before you make any travel arrangement. Find out if you would need any special documentation for traveling. Select the airline that can meet your flight requirements at non-busy times. Your child will be able to get more attention when the airline staff is not rushed.

Advise the reservation agent about the child's disability while booking your tickets. Let the agent know of the services you will need at the airport and on the airplane for the child. You can also call the airline later on if you bought the tickets online or through a travel agent. You must call the airline at least 48 hours before departure to ensure you will get the service and the equipment requested.

If your child has mobility issues, you can request wheelchair assistance at the airport. Wheelchair assistance will be available from the time you check in to the time you board the airplane. It will also be available at connection airports and at the destination airport. Call the airline 48 hours before your flight, to reserve wheelchair assistance. My daughter uses a large MacLaren Umbrella stroller designed for children with disabilities. However, I still reserve wheelchair assistance. This helps me get through security and often I can request assistance to get on and off the airplane.

Medical clearance may be required if your child has any neurological condition that causes seizures like epilepsy. If the child requires medical clearance for travel, obtain it from the doctor no more than 48 hours before travel. If your child has a medical device implanted in their body or is attached to the body like an insulin pump, check with the doctor if the child can go through the metal detector at the airport.

Request the meal most appropriate for the child, if meals are served during the flight.

Packing for the Trip

The regular limit of one carry-on and one personal item per traveler does not apply to medical equipment, and mobility/assistive devices carried by a person with a disability. The following is information on special items that you may be taking along:

Wheelchairs: If you child uses a special wheelchair and you are taking it along, it must go as check-in baggage. Prepare detailed instructions for disassembling and assembling the wheelchair and attach the instructions in a waterproof pouch to the wheelchair. This will enable the airline personnel to disassemble the wheelchair for storage. If the wheelchair is motorized, you must pack the batteries carefully in proper packaging. You can also request the airline to pack the batteries for you. This will require you to check-in at least an extra hour in advance.

Medication and prescriptions: Carry enough medication to last the entire trip and keep a copy of the prescription handy. Carry the medication in the original containers or packaging, if possible, and in a separate pouch to enable quick inspection. Pack the medication in the check-in bag and keep only the portion the child will require during the flight in the carry-on bag. The prescription may be required when going through customs and is useful to have in case you need to obtain more medication during the trip.

Prosthetic devices and related tools: The child can wear the prosthetic device during the travel. You can bring all the necessary tools that you require to remove or put on the prosthetic device in your carry-on bag.

At the Airport

Plan to arrive at the airport with extra time on hand. Do not check-in with a self-service kiosk. Check-in with the airline agent and advice them about the child's disability. Check with the agent that the child's ticket and the boarding pass has a note regarding any special services required. This note comes in very handy as you deal with different airline agents along your trip and you will not have to explain the disability of the child repeatedly. My daughter has a severe mobility disability and cannot even sit on her own. I have been on flights where I had to explain to every airline employee I met, what I needed for her. It was very frustrating.

Airport Security and Disability Specific Information

You can help the security officers at the airport do their job by cooperating with them. You should:

- ✓ Inform the officer about the child's special needs and if the security process may upset the child due to her disability.

- ✓ Suggest the best way to screen the child.

- ✓ Ask for help from the airline ground crew, security personnel, or flight attendants, especially if you are traveling alone with the child.

- ✓ Accompany the child if private screening is required and stay with the child at all times.

If your child has mobility disabilities:

- ✓ Let the security officers know the child's level of mobility and the use of any prosthetic device. They will adjust the screen process accordingly. For older children, you can request a private area for a pat-down inspection. Always accompany the child for any inspection.

- ✓ Security officers will inspect the child's wheelchair and perform explosive and trace detection test. The child does not need to be removed from the wheelchair for the inspection.

- ✓ Any equipment that can go through the x-ray machine should be placed on the x-ray belt.

If your child has hearing disabilities:

- ✓ Explain the security process to the child using sign language or any other means of communication, and help the security officer communicate with the child

- ✓ The child can wear a hearing device such as hearing aids as they go through security. These devices are not affected by X-ray inspection or metal detectors.

If your child has diabetes:

- ✓ Notify the security officer that your child has diabetes, if you are carrying diabetes related supplies for the child or the child has an insulin pump.

- ✓ Diabetes-related supplies allowed through security and on an airplane are insulin and insulin dispensing products, blood glucose testing products, insulin pump and pump supplies, and other related items. Insulin must be clearly labeled. Ideally, you should carry a note from the doctor about the insulin requirements. You can request a visual inspection of the diabetes related supplies and not put them through the x-ray machine.

✓ You can ask for pat-down inspection for the child if you do not want the child to go through the metal detector with an insulin pump.

The Flight

You and the child should pre-board. You can gate-check any equipment, like a folding wheelchair, that you cannot take into the cabin with you. If you have asked for wheelchair assistance, the wheelchair attendant will take the child to her seat on the airplane. You can then help her transfer from the wheelchair to her seat. Keep any medication or equipment you require during the flight in the seat pouch. Prepare the child for take-off.

You will have to assist the child to the restroom when the need arises. You will not have access to a wheelchair, once the flight is airborne. Choose a seat closer to the restroom, if this is a concern. You can also consider using diapers for the duration of the flight, depending on the child's mobility.

You will have access to a wheelchair once you reach your destination. You will have to wait for all the other passengers to leave the plane before the wheelchair attendant can bring the wheelchair on the plane to assist your child. If you gate-checked any equipment, you should get it when you get off the plane.

Traveling with a disabled child or a child with medical conditions is challenging and rewarding at the same time. The child is an important part of your life and traveling is another experience you can share and enjoy together. .

Chapter 10

Airport Security

Airport security is handled by the Transportation Security Administration (TSA), an agency operated by the federal government. This agency came into existence after the 9/11 attacks and aims to protect Americans at airports and in the air. The agency has put in place many policies and procedures, some of them controversial, to reach this aim. You can find detailed information on the TSA's website about airport security and screening procedures.

Getting Ready for Security

Getting children through security can be made a little easier with a little preparation. Get to know the latest security related rules and regulations from the TSA website before you begin packing. You have to pack your carry-on bags carefully, dress

Air Travel with Children

appropriately, and keep documentation handy to get through security as quickly as possible.

All carry-on baggage is screened, including diaper bags, strollers, umbrellas, etc. Any item that can go through the X-ray machine will be put through. If the item is too large, like an infant car seat, it will be checked manually by an officer. Tips to pack your carry-on bags:

- ✓ Pack the items in the bag in layers. Pack a layer of clothes, then electronics like charges and camera, then more clothes, and so on. This will enable the security officer to see what is in the bag as it goes through the X-ray machine.

- ✓ Do not pack your laptop or DVD player at the bottom of the bag. These items often have to be taken out of the bag and put in a separate container before they can go through the x-ray machine.

- ✓ Leave gifts unwrapped as they may need to be opened by the security officer to check the contents of the package

- ✓ If you have space in your carry-on bags, put all coats and jackets in there. You will have to take these off to go through security, even for the children, and that may take extra time.

- ✓ Pack all toiletries in clear, see-through zip-lock bags.

- ✓ Follow the 3-1-1 rule to pack liquids. Each passenger is allowed to bring 3.4 ounces of liquid or a 1-quart zip-lock bag with liquid or gel in his or her carry-on baggage. If you are carrying more liquid than that, pack it in your checked-in baggage. There are exceptions made to medications, baby formula, and special diets. You have to declare these items as you go through security.

✓ Do not pack any of the following in your carry-on bag:

- Sharp objects like knives, including Swiss army knives, box cutters, scissors, or knitting needles.

- Baseball bats, golf clubs.

- Fire arms of any type.

Check out Appendix 5 or the TSA website to get a full list of items that you can and cannot carry onboard.

Tips for Dressing:

✓ Avoid wearing clothes with metal attachments like buckles, large zippers, large decorative buttons, etc. You have to go through a metal detector at the airport. If an alarm sounds when you or the child goes through the detector, you would be subject to a pat-down inspection by the security officer. Other items that may set off the metal detectors are:

- Loose change, mobile phones

- Heavy jewelry
- Underwire bras
- Body piercings

✓ You are required to take off shoes before you go through the metal detector. Wear slip-on shoes that are quick to take-off and put on.

Documents to keep handy:

✓ Your boarding pass

✓ A government issued photo identification like a driver's license, passport, etc.

✓ Birth certificate, or a passport for the child – children are not required to show identification but I have found it never hurts to keep some documentation ready for the child, especially if you are traveling to a foreign country.

Going through Security

Arrive at the security checkpoint on time. Reserve at least half an hour to go through security. It takes longer to go through security at larger airports due to the large number of travelers.

TSA officers will not separate you from your child. They try to make the child as comfortable as possible as the child goes through security and will consult you if the child gets upset while going through screening. If a private screening is required, you would be allowed to escort the child and remain with him or her during the screening process. Here are the steps to follow while going through the metal detector:

- ✓ Empty your pockets and place the items in the small plastic containers provided by the airport security.

- ✓ Remove your laptop, if you are carrying one, from your carry-on bag and place it in the large container.

- ✓ Place your carry-on bags on the x-ray belt.

- ✓ Keep coats/jackets, shoes, etc. in another large container. Do not place these items over the laptop.

- ✓ Take the children out of the baby carrier or the stroller. The carrier and the stroller must go through the x-ray machine. Ask for help to fold the stroller, if you need to.

- ✓ If the children can walk, they should walk through the metal detector on their own. If you carry the child, you will both be screened by the security officer. Be prepared to help the security officer as he or she screens your child.

- ✓ Remove your bag of toiletries and place it in the container with the shoes

- ✓ Remove any baby formula or food that you may be carrying and give it to the security officer for inspection.

- ✓ If your child has special needs, inform the officer upfront. Suggest an alternative that will let the officers perform the screening without upsetting your child. If your child is in a wheelchair, you will not be asked to remove your child from the wheelchair. The child will be screened in the wheelchair and the wheelchair will be screened as well.

Other Air Security Tips

- ✓ Do not lock your check-in baggage. The lock may be broken by TSA to inspect your baggage. You can use one of the TSA approved locks, if you want to. TSA has the master key for these locks and can access the contents of the bag, without having to break the lock. You can buy TSA approved locks from <u>Safe Skies Luggage Locks</u> or <u>Travel Sentry</u>.

- ✓ I use bags with zippers. I usually secure the zipper with a plastic cable tie. I also keep a couple of ties in the bag with a note to the TSA officers, requesting that they put a new tie, if the bag is opened.

Tip — **Left something at the security checkpoint?**

Going through security takes time. You have to remove your watch, coat, belt, shoes, and other items and put these items through the x-ray machine. Sometimes you may forget to take items from all the different bins you may have used. You can contact the TSA Lost and Found office at the airport where you left the item. All items left at the security gate are forwarded to the Lost and Found office. If TSA is holding your item, you can send them a completed claim form with a prepaid self-addressed envelope large enough to fit the lost item.

You can find the TSA Lost and Found contact information for all airports in US at http://www.tsa.gov

Chapter 11

Infant Safety onboard

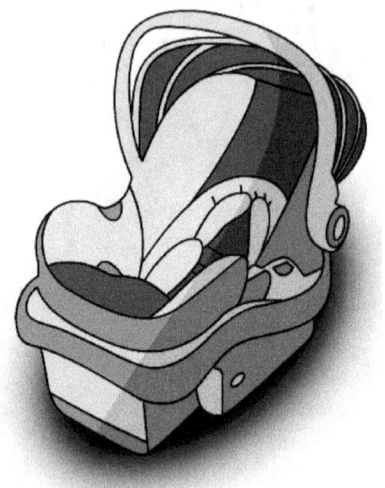

Airlines do not require you to buy a seat for children under than two years of age. Within the United States, Canada, Puerto Rico, and the U.S. Virgin Islands, an infant may be held in an adult's lap at no charge. If you are traveling to other countries, you may have to pay about 10% of the adult's fare for the infant held on your lap.

You are required to buy a seat for all children over the age of two. Airlines do not require you to use any type of special seat for the children.

FAA Recommendations

The Federal Aviation Administration (FAA) recommends that you buy a seat for your infant, and that the infant should travel in an approved child-restraining system (CRS). An example of a commonly used CRS is a car seat. FAA studies show that children are much safer in their own seat than on adult's lap during turbulence, take-off, and landing.

FAA has approved two types of CRS for use on airplanes. One is a hard-back child safety seat that can work as a car seat as well. The child safety seat should be rear facing for children less than 20 pounds and forward facing for children between 20 to 40 pounds. The other FAA-approved CRS is a harness-type restraint that may be used for children weighing between 22 and 44 pounds. The harness-type restraint can only be used on an airplane and is not is not approved for car use. All children over 40 pounds can use the airplane seat belt and do not require a CRS.

The FAA does not allow the use of booster seats, harness vests, and supplemental lap belts on airplanes.

Most car seats used today are usually acceptable for use in aircraft. If the seat is manufactured in US, it will carry a label such as "acceptable in all applicable federal motor vehicle safety standards" or "certified for use in motor vehicles and aircraft". If your child's car seat is manufactured in a foreign country, it would carry a similar label approved by either the United Nations or the government of the country where it was purchased.

Check your child's car seat for such a label before you take it with you to the airport. The car seat should not be more than 16 inches wide at the base. Car seats with a larger base will not fit in airplane seats, especially on small commuter planes. Airlines usually will not allow you to use a non-approved child restraining system. You may have to check-in your car seat, if not approved for airplane use, as baggage. Some airlines also provide their own CRS depending on the child's age if you have purchased a seat for the child. You could ask your airline if they provide a CRS and if you can bring your own.

Only way to ensure you will be able to use a CRS is purchasing a ticket. Ask your airline for a discounted fare. Many airlines now offer substantial discounts for children less than two years of age. If you are not purchasing a ticket, travel during non-busy times. If there is an empty seat next to you, the airline may let you use your CRS. Check with your airline for their specific policies.

Precautions with CRSs

Some important things to remember when using a CRS are:

- ✓ The CRS must be appropriate for the child according to his or her weight and age.
- ✓ The child-safety seat must be fitted in the airplane seat as per instructions on the seat label. It may face toward the front or rear of the plane. Fasten the airplane seat belt around the CRS as tightly as possible.

- ✓ The seat must not block any emergency exit on the airplane. It cannot be placed on an exit seat or the row in front of or behind an exit seat.

- ✓ The CRS may not be placed in an aisle seat. The best place for an infant safety seat is usually the window seat.

Using an Unapproved CRS

If you bring an unapproved child safety seat with you on the airplane, you will not be allowed to use it during taxi, takeoff, and landing, for safety reasons. You may be able to use it during the rest of the flight, depending on your airline's policy. I took my daughter's 'unapproved' car seat with me on the airplane and it fitted fine in the airplane seat. During take-off and landing the flight crew would not allow me to use it and I had to hold my daughter in my lap. However, I was free to use it for the rest of the ride. Find out about your airline's policy regarding regular car seats before bringing them onboard. Check them as baggage, if you are not allowed to use them at all during the flight.

Chapter 12

Health and Hygiene on the Plane

Children have delicate systems and can easily get sick. Airplane travel causes additional health concerns for  most parents. How will the children take to flying? Would they get motion sickness? Will they catch a cold from the other passengers? Would they be jet lagged? The following section explains airplane-related health concerns and steps parents can take to keep their children healthy.

Preventing Colds and Other Germs

An airplane's cabin contains a large number of people confined in a small space for a long time. The air is circulated through filters but this does not eliminate all the germs. If any passengers on the plane have a cold or some other airborne infection, you and the children are at risk of catching it.

Simple steps can help prevent the spread of infections:

- ✓ Stay hydrated throughout the flight: The mucous membranes in our nose filter the air we breathe and prevent viruses and germs from entering our body. The cabin air in the airplane is very dry and dries out the mucous membranes. Staying hydrated ensures that our nose can do its job filtering the air.

- ✓ Keep your hands clean: Wash your and children's hands when you visit the restroom. Carry instant hand sanitizer to keep hands clean during the flight

- ✓ Boost the body's immune system: Give the children an extra drink of orange juice for a few days before flying. Vitamin C strengthens the immune system and may help prevent a cold.

Travel Sickness

Many people suffer from airsickness or motion sickness. If you are flying with your children for the first time, you cannot be sure how they will react, although, if your children get sick in a car or on a boat, they would most probably get airsick too.

Motion sickness medication for children is available without a prescription, but you should consult your pediatrician if your child is taking some other medication on a regular basis. Motion sickness medication is also available in the form of a patch.

Motion sickness medication has to be taken prior to the flight, according to directions on the pack.

There are other products available for motion sickness such as wrist bands, herbal medication, etc. You can research these products on the internet, talk to you family and friends, and select a product that you think would suit you. I have tried the wristband but it did not work me – my friends swear by it.

If you know you suffer from motion sickness, do take some medication. You have to be in control on the airplane so that you can take care of your children. The children will be upset if they see you suffering from motion sickness.

If you travel well and the children have no symptoms of motion sick, do not give any medication. Keep it handy in case you need it. Carry some plastics bags to seal the sickness bags that you get on the airline.

Fear of Flying

Fear of flying is an anxiety phobia that may be related to heights, enclosed space, crowd, or some other cause. It may cause stress, weakness, dizziness, etc. Fear of flying is more common than most people realize. One out of every six Americans may show fear of flying to some degree. Some of these may be children.

Children usually develop a fear of flying either from experience, or by watching others act fearfully. For example, if someone close to the children starts crying every time airplanes are mentioned, the children may pick on it and develop the fear themselves. Children will not be afraid if this is their first trip.

You can help your child overcome the fear and even enjoy the flight. Talk about what it is they fear. Do not dismiss their fears – treat them seriously. Talk about the upcoming trip and all that it has to offer. Explain how you will help them navigate any issues that may arise. This may release any anxiety the children may be feeling about the trip. The following activities can comfort the children about flying and ease their worries:

- ✓ Read a book together where the main character goes on an enjoyable plane ride.

- ✓ Teach the children about how a plane flies. This information is available from various websites. Visit these websites with your children and make this information gathering fun. A list of children-friendly websites related to airplanes is available in the Resources section.

- ✓ If possible, visit the airport once before the actual trip.

Do not behave fearfully in front of the children if you do not enjoy flying or are afraid yourself. If you have any concerns about the upcoming trip, do not talk about them to the children or within their earshot. Be positive.

Keep the children happy and busy at the airport and during the flight. Do not give them an opportunity to dwell on their fears.

Dehydration

Air inside the airplanes is drier than desert air. The air tends to get drier as the length of the flight increases. You and the children could get dehydrated when you travel over long distances. Basic symptoms of dehydration are thirst, dry and/or wrinkled skin, constipation, scratchy eyes, etc. During the flight, the nostrils can dry up and it can get very uncomfortable. You all need to drink plenty of water to hydrate yourselves, not just during the flight, but also after landing. To keep hydrated:

- ✓ Make sure all of you drink plenty of water. Keep bottles and sippy cups filled with water and encourage the children to take sips regularly during the flight

- ✓ Drink juices offered to you as part of the cabin service.

- ✓ You should avoid alcohol and coffee; they have diuretic properties and can worsen dehydration.

- ✓ Cover your nose with a wet handkerchief. This will saturate your nostrils, but looks odd on an airplane. Children do not respond well to a wet cloth on their face. Alternatively, you can apply some olive oil or almond oil to the nostrils before flying. This will prevent the nostrils from drying up.

- ✓ After landing, take a shower or bath as soon as possible. It will not only reduce tiredness but also hydrate your body.

Do not drink tap water on the plane. There are currently no standards governing the cleanliness of the water carried by planes and you have no idea what type of water you will get. Ask for bottled water or carry your own. You may buy bottled water after you go through security.

Using Sedatives

When I was traveling for the first time with my daughter, I was advised by many well-meaning folks that I should carry some sedatives like Benadryl with me. I could give it to my daughter about half hour before the flight and then she will sleep through the flight.

The idea was very tempting initially. However, I decided against it after talking to my pediatrician. The Pediatrician told me that I could use it, but that she really did not feel it was necessary. She also warned me that some children become hyperactive with the medication so I should try it out first a couple of days before the flight. I thought it through and then decided not to use it. I had everything that could make my daughter comfortable and I really did not know how she would behave on the plane. She has always enjoyed car rides and easily falls asleep in the car. I was hoping this would work on the plane as well. I carried the medicine with me anyway, just for good luck.

You will have to make your own decision about giving your children sedatives. There are two main types of sedatives:

✓ An antihistamine such like Benadryl

✓ A strong sedative

You can buy antihistamines over the counter, but the sedatives are available mostly by prescription only. Both these types of sedatives can make some children hyperactive and may cause nightmares. Talk to your children's pediatrician about your options. This is especially important if your infant is taking any other medicine on a regular basis. The pediatrician can also suggest the correct dosage based on your children's age and weight. You may have to try the medication two or three days in advance to find out how your children react to the medication.

Do not take any sedatives yourself – you have to be in control to look after your child.

> **Info** **Benadryl and my daughter**
>
> I did not give my daughter, Betu, Benadryl on her first flight. She was six months old at the time. I had thought that the humming of the plan engine would put her to sleep, but that did not happen. The plane was too noisy for her and she just could not sleep. I gave her Benadryl on the flight back. That did not work out either. It was about a two-hour flight and by the time the Benadryl took effect, we were halfway through the flight. She woke up as the plane started to descend, was groggy and could not go back to sleep, crying for a long time afterwards.
>
> Over the next few trips, I realized that a sedative is an option for my daughter only on long flights, that is, flights over four hours. She is then able to sleep through a large part of the flight and does not wake up groggy. As she has grown older, she has also learnt to deal with the changes in the air pressure, and the flight descent is no longer a problem.

Avoiding Ear Pressure Problems

Airplane cabins are pressurized, but the pressure changes during takeoff and landing. Most people can feel the change in pressure in their ears, but for some it can be extremely uncomfortable and even painful.

Here are some tips to make sure your children are comfortable during take-off and landing:

- ✓ If your children have a head cold, see if it can be cleared before you start traveling.

- ✓ If your children take a bottle or are breast-fed, offer them the bottle or the breast as the case may be. You can offer a drink from a straw cup to the older children. The act of swallowing can relieve ear pressure.

- ✓ Talk to your older children about what to expect before the flight take-off. Explain to them what is ear pressure and what they may experience. Reassure them that this is completely normal and will not last long.

- ✓ Offer the older children gummy candy to suck.

- ✓ Ask the flight attendant for ear plugs when you board. Put these in the children's ears before the flight takes off. Children usually do not keep them on for long, but they can be very helpful

- ✓ Yawning can also help relieve air pressure.

If your children have an ear infection, you should discuss the trip with your pediatrician. Ear infections can be extremely painful during a plane ride. In severe cases, it may be advisable not to fly until the infection has cleared. You should get your children's ears checked a couple of days before the flight. Flying with an ear infection can cause permanent damage to the eardrums.

Jet Lag

The body has a built-in system to keep track of time and regulate sleep, hunger, and body temperature accordingly. The body uses sunlight as a guide for this timekeeping. When you travel across time zones, the body's built-in timekeeping system goes out-of-sync. The body requires time to adjust to this new time cycle and is "jet lagged". Jet lag is considered a medical condition and is referred to as "desynchronosis".

The major symptoms of jet lag are headache, nausea, irregular sleeping patterns, temporary insomnia, fatigue, digestive issues, etc. The intensity of the symptoms depends on the distance traveled and number of time zone crossed. Crossing one or two time zones does not cause jet lag. A person traveling from north to south, like Boston to Miami, will be tired but will not be "jet lagged" as there is no change in time zones. Traveling from east to west (New York to Los Angeles) has less jet lag symptoms than traveling from west to east. The more time zones you cross, the worse the jet lag.

The intensity of jet lag symptoms and the amount of time required to recover varies from person to person. Some people may require several days to adjust to a new time zone, while others experience little disruption. There are multiple remedies for jet lag. You will have to find out what works best for you and your children. Here are the most common ways to cut down on jet lag:

- ✓ Avoid alcohol and caffeine before and during travel. These drinks dehydrate the body and can worsen jet lag.

- ✓ Try to sleep on the plane, especially if you are traveling west to east (LA to New York).

- ✓ Move around the plane. Stretch your legs and encourage the children to do the same. However, do not let the children run up and down the aisle and disturb other passengers.

- ✓ Drink plenty of water on the plane and after you reach your destination.

- ✓ Take a shower when you get to your destination. This will freshen you up and reduce jet lag.

- ✓ Eat more carbohydrates for increased energy.

- ✓ Get some sun – walk outside and absorb sunlight as soon as you get a chance.

- ✓ Get some exercise. This does not have to be strenuous exercise. Take the children out for a quick walk around the beach, garden, or hotel.

- ✓ Avoid afternoon naps. If children get sleepy at odd times, try to divert their attention. Take them for a walk; go have an ice cream, play games. Sleeping at odd times increases the time the body takes to recover from jet lag.

- ✓ Use melatonin – sleeping through the night is the best way to get over jet lag-related fatigue. This will allow the children to get a full night's sleep and wake up rested and ready to go. Please note that the use of melatonin has not been approved by the Food and Drug Administration Agency. You should talk to your doctor before giving this or any other medicine to your children. Avoid sleeping pills on the plane. You want to be in control at all times be able to take care of your children.

✓ Take a No-Jet-Lag tablet – I have not used these but many people find them very effective. These are available for children as well. Do talk to your doctor about any possible side effects.

All these remedies can help with reducing jet lag but will not eliminate it. You have to give the body time to adjust to the new time zone and schedule. Try to fit into your plans at least a day or two to recover from jet lag. Keep the schedule for the first day or two light. Remember that well rested children are happy and cooperative.

Alternative Health Remedies

Alternative health remedies can help you recover faster from the flight. Here are some common uses:

✓ Back Flower Remedy spray may be used for stress relief.

✓ Aromatherapy oils, like lavender oil, may also be used, for their calming effect. You may apply it to your wrist or on a tissue before, during, or after the flight.

- ✓ 'No-Jet-Lag' tablets may be used during the flight to avoid being jet lagged when you arrive at your destination.

- ✓ Take an extra dose of vitamin C or a supplement like Airborne before or after the flight to boost your body's immune system. Chinese herbal supplements, like Astragalus, may also be taken before the flight to boost the immune system.

- ✓ Ginger Ale may be used for motion sickness

Your Medical Kit

Keep a small medical kit ready with you at all times. This will help cover any emergency that may arise at the airport or during the flight. I like this kit to contain only bare essentials, and pack the rest in the checked-in luggage. Here are my suggestions:

- ✓ Any medication that your children are taking: keep enough medication that is required during travel plus some extra, in case the flight gets delayed. If the medicine is essential, keep the whole supply at hand.

- ✓ 5-10 band-aids: I keep the printed colorful ones and use some of them for playing games.

- ✓ Saline nose drops to keep the nostrils hydrated.

- ✓ Pain/fever medicine like Acedamopine.

- ✓ Sedative for the children, if you are planning to use some or want some, just in case

- ✓ Motion sickness medicine

- ✓ Antiseptic cream (small tube)

I keep a full first-aid kit in the checked-in baggage and it is ready to use when we get to our destination.

Chapter 13

Entertainment Onboard

Children cannot sit still – you know that. They do not sit still at home and are not going to on the airplane. It is your job to make sure that the children are comfortable and do not disturb other passengers. Be prepared to keep them entertained and busy on the flight.

Contrary to popular belief, I find that infants are the easiest to handle among all age groups. Yes, they may cry when they are upset or uncomfortable, but often sleep through the majority of the flight. A few simple items like 2-3 colorful rattles with gentle sounds, a favorite blanket, and a pacifier are usually enough to keep them happy. Make sure that the infant is comfortable. Change and feed the infant on time according to your regular schedule and let them nap when they want.

Toddlers are the hardest to handle. They want to move constantly and get fidgety when they cannot do so. You have to keep them diverted and busy throughout the flight. Children do get easier to handle, as they grow older. Here are some tips that may help

Pack toys in your carry-on bags

- ✓ Allow the toddlers to bring one or two of their favorite toys onboard. These toys should not contain liquids like water or make loud noises.

- ✓ Buy a new toy for the toddler and give it to them on the plane. The new toy will grab their attention for a while as they explore it and learn to play with it.

Bring activity or picture books

- ✓ Read books to the children on the plane.

- ✓ Let them look at the pictures or give them a coloring book with one or two crayons. Do not give them a whole pack of crayons – the pack would end up on the floor and the roll away. You do not want to be diving under the seat to search for small items.

- ✓ Get a new book. It will be a new thing to explore just like the new toy.

- ✓ Bring puzzle books for the older children. Books with simple puzzles work best as they keep the children mentally engaged.

In-flight Entertainment

More and more flights have built-in television screens in the headrest of the seat in front of you and offer a selection of movies, shows, and games. Check out what your flight has to offer ahead of time from the airline website. Depending on the selection on your fight, this can be a good option for you to entertain the children during the flight. You do not even have to lug a portable DVD player and each child can enjoy a different program.

Portable DVD Players

If your flight is long or does not have appropriate entertainment options for the children, bring your portable DVD player with few of their favorite DVDs. Get one or two new DVDs that the children have not watched yet.

Family Time

As you are all seated together in a confined space, this is an ideal opportunity for some quality family time. Talk to your children and encourage them to tell you about what is happening at school, the playground, etc. Tell them about what to expect when they get to their destination. If they are going to meet family members, show them pictures of the people they are going to meet and tell them something interesting (and appropriate) about each family member they are going to meet. If you are going to a holiday destination, tell them about that destination.

Playing Games

Play games with the children to pass the time. For example, babies love to play peek-a-boo, listen to nursery rhymes, be tickled, etc. With older children, you could play games like storytelling, "I spy", or some other game that they like. Make a list ahead of time of games that you think would work on the plane.

Airline Activity Kits

Some airlines provide activity kits for small children, especially on long flights. Usually, it is a small bag with 2-3 small toys, a coloring book with a couple of crayons, and other items. It is like a tiny treasure for the children as they go through the bag and figure out what to do with each item. The flight attendant will usually hand out the activity kit after the flight has taken off.

Take your toddler around the plane (without disturbing other passengers)

You can take your toddlers down the aisle to the back of the airplane and show them around the airplane. Let them say "hello" and wave to other passengers. This is especially helpful in long flights as this entertains the children and gives them an opportunity to move around the airplane. Do not do this when the attendants are serving food or drinks, or are moving carts down the aisles. Make sure that you toddler does not disturb other passengers.

Have fun with your children. Your attitude will set the tone. If you relax and seem to enjoy yourself, the children will enjoy themselves too. This is their first airplane ride. The more they enjoy the trip, the easier it will be for you in the future. The other travelers around you will also appreciate it if you keep the children busy and happy.

Toy Suggestions

Selecting which toys to take with you and which to leave behind is not easy. The toys should be appropriate for use on the airplane, and anywhere else you will be going during your vacation. You know your children the best and know what keeps them happy. Here are some options, listed according to age category. Choose entertainment that will work best for your child. The toys should be light and sturdy. This will minimize the chances of them breaking apart in mid-flight and you will have less weight to carry. Any toys, that you may not be able to use at the airport and on the airplane, should be packed in checked-in bags.

Toys for Infants

- ✓ Rattles and Musical toys with soft sounds - you do not want to disturb your fellow passengers with loud and shrill noises.

- ✓ Bright colored soft toys

- ✓ Plastic mirrors

- ✓ Infant's favorite blanket (if there is one).

Older Babies and Toddlers

- ✓ Blanket or stuffed animal (for comfort)
- ✓ Board or sensory books
- ✓ Dolls or stuffed toys
- ✓ Portable CD/DVD players with their favorite CDs/DVDs

Young Children (Pre-School, Kindergarten)

- ✓ Etch-a-Sketch or an erasable slate with attached pen or a similar toy
- ✓ Picture or activity books with crayons: give only one crayon to the child at a time
- ✓ Plastic toys (dolls, animals, dinosaurs, cars, and others)
- ✓ Play dough
- ✓ Portable CD/DVD players with their favorite CDs/DVDs

Older Children

- ✓ Books and comics for reading
- ✓ Card games like playing cards, Pokémon cards – These tend to get dropped on the airplane floor

and lost, so are best used while waiting for the flight in the airport.

- ✓ Hand-held video or electronic games
- ✓ Portable CD/DVD players with their favorite CDs/DVDs
- ✓ Puzzle books like Sudoku, word games, crosswords, etc.

Chapter 14

Nowhere to Go

Any airplane traveler's biggest nightmare is being stuck at an airport in the middle of nowhere. The nightmare becomes worse, if you are traveling with small children. Flight delays and cancellations are common. According to the Department of Transportation's Air Travel Consumer Report's data, almost one in four domestic flights is late.

Fortunately, most delays are less than one hour. They are an inconvenience, but can be handled as part of the travel experience. Dealing with longer flight delays or flight cancellations is a bigger problem. Weather is the biggest culprit when it comes to long delays and cancellations.

This chapter offers suggestions on making the best of your time if you are unfortunate enough to be stuck in the airport and on getting some compensation from the airlines.

Avoid Getting Stuck at the Airport

You can take simple steps to avoid getting stuck in the first place. These steps do not work all the time but can help you avoid long airport stays the majority of times.

- ✓ Check if your flight and connecting flights, if any, are on time before you leave for the airport.

- ✓ If your current flight is late, do you have ample time to make the connection? Arrange for an alternative connecting flight before you leave, when you know that your original connection will be almost impossible to make.

- ✓ Check the weather at your destination and the airport where you will change planes.

- ✓ Airlines often let you change your ticket reservations at no cost if there is a weather advisory that will affect your itinerary. Check with the airline and rebook your flight for a better connection if your travel is not of an urgent nature.

Again, these steps will not guarantee that you will not have to spend a night in the airport, but will substantially reduce the possibility.

Making Alternative Arrangements

First things come first! Once you realize your flight is delayed or cancelled, the first thing to do is to keep your cool and make alternative arrangements. If you get upset or angry, the children will read your cues, and become restless and harder to control.

Cause of the Flight Delay

Find out all you can about the flight delay. Find out the cause. Airlines do not always announce the cause of the delay or cancellation but will tell you if you ask. Talk to the airline representative and find out the cause of the delay or the flight cancellation.

Tip	Call the airlines toll free information number. Often you can get better and up-to-date information from the toll free line and you may be able to make changes to your reservations quickly and easily.

If your cancellation is caused by the airline, due to a mechanical failure, for example, you should be able to negotiate future travel discount vouchers, meal vouchers and even hotel accommodations if you are delayed overnight. If the cancellation is because of bad weather, however, you may not get much help from the airline.

Arranging for Another Flight

If your flight is delayed, find out how long is the delay and plan accordingly. Do not leave for the airport if you know that your flight is late. Flight delays may impact your connections. Do not take the first flight unless you know you will make the connection or have alternative arrangements.

If your flight has been cancelled, find out when the next flight that the airline can accommodate you on is due. The flight may be operated by the same airline or a different airline. Will your airline endorse your ticket so that you can fly with another airline, if it has space available?

Remember, all the passengers who were going on your flight are doing the same thing, so you have to be proactive and talk to the airline representative as soon as you can. Alternatively, you can call your travel agent. The travel agent has access to more information than you do about all the flights that may be an option for you. They can find the best solution for you and change your reservations. If you are on a non-stop flight that is cancelled, your travel agent may be able to put you on a flight with confirmed connections that will get you to your destination. Airline staff at the airport rarely offers you such options.

The cost can vary depending on where you bought the ticket, the class of tickets, airline rules, etc. If you originally bought the ticket through the travel agent, these changes might cost you considerably less.

Tracking your Bags

If you have checked-in your bags and you have to change flights due to delays or cancellation, your bags may not get to your destination with you. Keep your baggage claim tags handy and call the airlines to make sure your bags get to your destination, even if they get there on a different flight. The airline will deliver the bags to your home or hotel at no cost when the bags arrive.

Getting a Refund

If your flight is cancelled due to the airline's error or a mechanical problem, you are entitled to a full refund, even on a non-refundable ticket. You should put in a request for a refund as soon as possible. The airline may not give you a cash refund, but will issue you vouchers that you can use for travel in the future (within 2 years). You may be able to get travel vouchers of some value even if your flight has been cancelled due to weather conditions.

Making Arrangements for an Overnight Stay

If you were traveling alone you could have spent the night hanging on the baggage cart. However, you are traveling with young children; you should arrange for somewhere to stay if you know that you are not leaving until the next day. Here are some options:

- ✓ Check if the airline has a lounge in the airport that they will let you use. Airport lounges are open usually for business and first class passengers only. You may be able to get in if you carry certain credit cards, or there may be a charge to use the lounge.

- ✓ Call hotels and motels near the airport to find a room. Hotels that are close to the airport are usually more expensive. Do not expect a discount if multiple flights have been cancelled due to weather conditions. Even hotels within the high price range will be filling up quickly, so make your move quickly if want to spend the night in comfort.

- ✓ If you cannot get a hotel room and have to spend the night in the airport, find a quiet corner such as an empty gate area and feel free to spread out. Spread out the blanket and let the children rest on it. Keep children busy with games, talk to them, and tire them out. Tired children will sleep anywhere. The most important thing to remember is to maintain your cheerfulness. Children are very adaptable and can relax and enjoy themselves in different environments if you are not anxious.

Remember that losing your cool and getting upset will not help anybody.

Spending Time at the Airport

You can get a good idea of how long you will be spending at the airport after you have found out the cause of the delay and arranged alternative flights. Hopefully, there will not be any further delays to your flight. You can turn this time at the airport with your children into quality time. You can do many activities together at the airport and have some fun. Keeping busy will also help the time go faster and make waiting for the flight easier.

Get to know the Airport

Large airports have many more activities to offer than small or regional airports. Find out about the airport. How many terminals does the airport have and how can you go from terminal to terminal? Find out what is at each terminal. Most terminals will have different restaurants and food choices. Usually there is a free shuttle to take you around the airport terminals. Go for a ride around the airport terminals. You can get off at the terminal of your choice and take walk around or have a meal. This is easier if you have checked-in your luggage and only have the carry-on items. Most large airports have lockers for hire. You can rent a locker and store the baggage, if the check-in option is not available for your flight. If you have already gone through security, you will have to go out to go around the terminals and then go through the security process again.

Some airports have a children's play area, usually in the main terminal. If your gate area is close to it, you can take children there. It will distract them if the flight is delayed for a short while. Many airports also have an "infant area" with changing tables, a feeding area, and restrooms for infants and toddlers. You can change and feed the children here as you wait. Find out if there is an airline lounge that you can use. Take the children to the lounge if they need a quiet place to rest.

Explore the airport with the children, within your available time. Airports often have aviation galleries with pictures displaying the history of the airport and the city, or artwork on display. They may have observation decks, where you can watch flights take-off and land.

Take Care of Yourself

Eating is most important. Find out your food options and select one that best suits your needs. Avoid alcoholic drinks as they will tire you out quickly. Get some candy to indulge the children later.

Some airports have good shower facilities. You can shower or let older children shower, especially if you have had a long first flight and are waiting for the next one. This will relax you and leave you refreshed and energized.

Passing Time at the Airport

It's all about the attitude. You are in the airport and you are not going anywhere until your flight takes off, so play with the children and show them how to have fun. Some options are:

- ✓ Play with the games you brought along to play on the flight.

- ✓ Listen to music on your iPod or CD player.

- ✓ Watch movies on your portable DVD player or laptop, if you have brought one.

- ✓ Buy a disposable camera and give it to the children. Let them snap pictures of things around the gate area or where you may be seated.

- ✓ Count airplanes that you can see from the window, people at the gate, or stores in the terminal, etc.

- ✓ Work on an activity book (which you can get at the airport convenience store.)

- ✓ Read books to the children.

- ✓ Tell them stories – you can even make-up a story along with the children. Toddlers have an active imagination and love story telling.

- ✓ Find a quiet corner, where the children can have a nap. Spread out the blanket and let them take a nap on it.

- ✓ Play cards – you can buy a pack of playing cards at the airport convenience store

- ✓ Window shop at the airport. Large airports have big shopping areas with many attractions. These are expensive but fun to visit. I did this when my daughter was an infant. It became harder as she became more active.

- ✓ Get an Internet connection for the older children. The Internet can keep them occupied for hours.

Do let the children know that you are having fun. They will appreciate that.

Appendices

Appendix 1: List of Airlines

Here is a list all major airlines that fly within US, and to and from US.

A

Airline Information	Reservations Number	Website
AccessAir	800-307-4984	http://www.accessair.net/
Action Airlines	800-243-8623	http://www.actionairlines.com/
Aer Lingus	800-474-7424	http://www.aerlingus.com/
Aeroflot	888-340-6400	http://www.aeroflot.com/
Aero Honduras	800-333-0276	http://www.aerohonduras.com
Aerolineas Argentinas	800-333-0276	http://www.aerolineas.com.ar/
AeroLitoral	800-237-6639	http://www.aerolitoral.com/
Aeromar	877-237-6627	http://www.flyaeromar.com/
Aeromexico	800-237-6639	http://www.aeromexico.com/
Aeropostal	888-912-8466	http://www.aeropostal.com/
Afrinat Airlines	866-359-7111	http://www.afrinat.com/
Air Baltic	800-548-8181	http://www.airbaltic.com/
Air Botswana	800-518-7781	http://www.airbotswana.co.bw/
Air Canada	888-247-2262	http://www.aircanada.ca/
Air Caraibes	877-772-1005	http://www.aircaraibes.com/
Air China	800-986-1985	http://www.airchina.com.cn/
Air Europa	800-238-7672	http://www.air-europa.com/
Air Fiji	877-247-3454	http://www.airfiji.net/
Air France	800-237-2747	http://www.airfrance.com/
Air India	800-223-7776	http://www.airindia.com/
Air Jamaica	800-523-5585	http://www.airjamaica.com/
Air Labrador	800-563-3042	http://www.airlabrador.com/
Air Lanka	800-421-9898	http://www.srilankan.aero/

Air Madagascar	800-821-3388	http://www.airmadagascar.mg/
Air Malta	800-756-2582	http://www.airmalta.com/
Air Mauritius	800-363-9675	http://www.airmauritius.com/
Air Midwest	800-428-4322	http://www.midwestairlines.com/MAWeb/
Air Namibia	800-626-4242	http://www.airnamibia.com.na/
Air New Zealand	800-262-1234	http://www.airnewzealand.com/
Air Niugini	714-752-5440	http://www.airniugini.com.pg/
Air North	800-764-0407	http://www.flyairnorth.com/
Air Pacific	800-227-4446	http://www.airpacific.com/
Air Paraguay	800-577-7771	N/A
Air Santo Domingo	888-359-2772	http://airsantodomingo.com.do/
Air St. Thomas	800-522-3084	http://www.airstthomas.com/
Air Sunshine	800-327-8900	http://www.airsunshine.com/
Air Tahiti Nui	877-824-4846	http://www.airtahitinui.com/
Air Transat	877-872-6728	http://www.airtransat.com/
Air Vanuatu	800-677-4277	http://www.airvanuatu.com/
Air Vegas Airlines	800-255-7474	http://www.airvegas.com/
Air Zimbabwe	800-742-3006	http://www.airzimbabwe.com/
AirTran Airways	800-247-8726	http://www.airtran.com/
Airzena Georgian Airlines	800-220-3106	http://www.airzena.com/
Alaska Airlines	800-252-7522	http://www.alaskaair.com/
Alaska Seaplane Service	800-478-3360	http://www.akseaplanes.com/
Alitalia	800-223-5730	http://www.alitalia.com/
All Nippon Airways	800-235-9262	http://www.ana.co.jp/
Allegheny Airlines	800-428-4322	http://www.alleghenyairlines.com/
Allegiant Air	888-594-6937	http://www.allegiant-air.com/
Aloha Airlines	800-367-5250	http://www.alohaairlines.com/
America West	800-235-9292	http://www.americawest.com/
American Airlines	800-433-7300	http://www.aa.com/
American Eagle	800-433-7300	http://www.aa.com/
Arctic Circle Air Service	888-414-2364	http://www.arctic-circle-air.com/
Arizona Express Airlines	866-435-9872	http://www.azxpress.com/
Asiana Airlines	800-227-4262	http://www.flyasiana.com/

Appendix 1

ATA Airlines	800-435-9282	http://www.ata.com/
Atkin Air	800-924-2471	http://www.atkinair.com/
Atlantic Airlines	800-879-0000	http://www.atlanticairlines.com/
Atlantic Southeast Airlines	800-282-3424	http://www.flyasa.com/
Australian Airlines	800-227-4500	http://www.australianairlines.com.au/
Austrian Airlines	800-843-0002	http://www.aua.com/
Aviacsa	888-528-4227	http://www.aviacsa.com.mx/
Avianca	800-284-2622	http://www.avianca.com/

B

Airline Information	Reservations Number	Website
Bahamasair	800-222-4262	http://www.bahamasair.com/
Bangkok Airways	866-226-4565	http://www.bangkokair.com/
Baxter Aviation	800-661-5599	http://www.baxterair.com/
Bearskin Airlines	800-465-2327	http://www.bearskinairlines.com/
Bering Air	800-478-5422	http://www.beringair.com/
Big Sky Airlines	800-237-7788	http://www.bigskyair.com/
Bmi	800-788-0555	http://www.flybmi.com/
Boston-Maine Airways	800-359-7262	http://www.bmairways.com/
British Airways	800-247-9297	http://www.britishairways.com/
British Mediterranean Airways	800-247-9297	http://www.britishmediterranean.com/
Bulgaria Air	800-852-0944	http://www.air.bg/
BWIA West Indies Airways	800-538-2942	http://www.bwee.com/

C

Airline Information	Reservations Number	Website
Calm Air	800-839-2256	http://www.calmair.com/
Cape Air	800-352-0714	http://www.flycapeair.com/

Airline	Reservations Number	Website
Caribbean Star Alliance	866-864-6272	http://www.flycaribbeanstar.com/
Caribbean Sun Airlines	866-864-6272	http://www.flycsa.com/
Cathay Pacific	800-233-2742	http://www.cathaypacific.com/
Cayman Airways	800-422-9626	http://www.caymanairways.com/
Chalk's Ocean Airways	800-424-2557	http://www.flychalks.com/
Champion Air	800-387-6951	http://www.championair.com/
Chicago Express Airlines	800-435-9282	http://www.chicagoexpress.com/
China Airlines	800-227-5118	http://www.china-airlines.com/
China Eastern Airlines	800-200-5118	http://www.ce-air.com/
China Southern Airlines	888-338-8988	http://www.cs-air.com/
Colgan Air	800-272-5488	http://www.colganair.com/
Comair	800-727-2550	http://www.comair.com/
CommutAir	800-525-0280	http://www.commutair.com/
Condor Flugdienst	800-524-6975	http://www.condor.com/
Continental Airlines	800-523-3273	http://www.continental.com/
Copa Airlines	800-FLY-COPA	http://www.copaair.com/
Corporate Airlines	800-555-6565	http://www.corporateairlines.com/
CSA Czech Airlines	877-293-4225	http://www.czechairlines.com/
Cyprus Airways	800-966-4274	http://www.cyprusairways.com/

D

Airline Information	Reservations Number	Website
Delta Air Lines	800-221-1212	http://www.delta.com/
Dragonair	800-233-2742	http://www.dragonair.com/

E

Airline Information	Reservations Number	Website
EgyptAir	800-334-6787	http://www.egyptair.com.eg/
El Al	800-223-6700	http://www.elal.co.il/
Emirates	800-777-3999	http://www.emirates.com/
Era Aviation	800-866-8394	http://www.flyera.com/
Estonian Air	800-397-1354	http://www.estonian-air.ee/
Ethiopian Airlines	800-445-2733	http://www.ethiopianairlines.com/
EVA Air	800-695-1188	http://www.evaair.com/

F

Airline Information	Reservations Number	Website
Finnair	800-950-5000	http://www.finnair.com/
First Air	800-267-1247	http://www.firstair.ca/
Florida Coastal Airlines	888-435-9322	http://www.floridacoastalairlines.com/
Forward Air	800-726-6654	http://www.forwardair.com/
Frontier Airlines	800-432-1359	http://www.frontierairlines.com/
Frontier Flying Service	800-478-6779	http://www.frontierflying.com/

G

Airline Information	Reservations Number	Website
Garuda Indonesia	800-342-7832	http://www.garuda-indonesia.com/
Grand Canyon Airlines	866-235-9422	http://www.grandcanyonairlines.com/
Great Lakes Airlines	800-554-5111	http://www.greatlakesav.com/

Great Plains Airlines	866-929-8646	http://www.greatplainsairlines.com/
Gulf Air	800-553-2824	http://www.gulfairco.com/
Gulfstream Airlines	800-525-0280	http://www.gulfstreamair.com/

H

Airline Information	Reservations Number	Website
Harbour Air Ltd.	800-665-0212	http://www.harbour-air.com/home/index.php
Harmony Airways	866-868-6789	http://www.harmonyairways.com/
Hawaiian Airlines	800-367-5320	http://www.hawaiianair.com/
Hawkair	866-429-5247	http://www.hawkair.net/
Helijet	800-665-4354	http://www.helijet.com/
Horizon Air	800-547-9308	http://www.horizonair.com/

I

Airline Information	Reservations Number	Website
Iberia	800-772-4642	http://www.iberia.com/
Icelandair	800-223-5500	http://www.icelandair.net/
Independence Air	800-FLY-FLYi	http://www.flyi.com/
Indigo	877-446-3446	http://www.flyindigo.com/
Island Air	800-323-3345	http://www.islandair.com/

J

Airline Information	Reservations Number	Website
Japan Airlines	800-525-3663	http://www.jal.com/
Jazz (Air Canada)	888-247-2262	http://www.flyjazz.ca/
JetBlue Airways	800-538-2583	http://www.jetblue.com/

K

Airline Information	Reservations Number	Website
Kenmore Air	866-435-9524	http://www.kenmoreair.com/
Kenya Airways	866-536-9224	http://www.kenya-airways.com/
Keystone Air Service	800-665-3975	http://www.keystoneair.mb.ca/
KLM	800-447-4747	http://www.klm.com/
Korean Air	800-438-5000	http://www.koreanair.com/
Kuwait Airways	800-458-9248	http://www.kuwait-airways.com/

L

Airline Information	Reservations Number	Website
LAB Airlines	800-337-0918	http://www.labairlines.com/
Lan Airlines	866-435-9526	http://www.lan.com/
LanDominicana	800-735-5526	http://www.landominicana.com/
LanEcuador	800-735-5526	http://www.lanecuador.com/
LanPeru	800-526-7378	http://www.lanperu.com/
Liat Airlines	868-624-4727	http://www.liatairline.com/
Lithuanian Airlines	877-454-8482	http://www.lal.lt/
Lloyd Aereo Boliviano	800-337-0918	http://www.labairlines.com/
LOT Polish Airlines	800-223-0593	http://www.lot.com/
LTU	866-266-5588	http://www.ltu.de/
Lufthansa	800-645-3880	http://www.lufthansa.com/

M

Airline Information	Reservations Number	Website
Malaysia Airlines	800-552-9264	http://www.malaysiaairlines.com.my/

Airline Information	Reservations Number	Website
Malev Hungarian Airlines	800-223-6884	http://www.malev.hu/
Martinair	800-627-8462	http://www.martinair.com/
Maya Island Air	800-225-6732	http://www.mayaairways.com/
Mesa Airlines	800-637-2247	http://www.mesa-air.com/
Mesaba Airlines	800-225-2525	http://www.mesaba.com/
Mexicana	800-531-7921	http://www.mexicana.com/
MIAT - Mongolian Airlines	800-642-8768	http://www.miat.com/
Midwest Airlines	800-452-2022	http://www.midwestairlines.com/

N

Airline Information	Reservations Number	Website
Nationwide Airlines	866 686-6558	http://www.flynationwide.co.za/
Nature Air	800-235-9272	http://www.natureair.com/
Northwest Airlines	800-225-2525	http://www.nwa.com/

O

Airline Information	Reservations Number	Website
Olson Air Service	800-478-5600	N/A
Olympic Airlines	800-223-1226	http://www.olympicairlines.com/
Omni Air International	877-718-8901	http://www.omniairintl.com/

P

Airline Information	Reservations Number	Website
Pacific Wings	888-575-4546	http://www.pacificwings.com/

Pakistan International Airlines	800-578-6786	http://www.piac.com.pk/
Pan Am	800-359-7262	http://www.flypanam.com/
Papillon Airways	800-528-2418	http://www.papillon.com/
Peace Air	800-563-3060	http://www.peaceair.com/
Pen Air	800-448-4226	http://www.penair.com/
Philippine Airlines	800-435-9725	http://www.philippineair.com/
Piedmont Airlines	800-428-4322	http://www.piedmont-airlines.com/
Pinnacle Airlines	800-225-2525	http://www.nwairlink.com/
Polynesian Airlines	800-264-0823	http://www.polynesianairlines.com/
Promech Air	800-860-3845	http://www.promechair.com/

Q

Airline Information	Reservations Number	Website
Qantas	800-227-4500	http://www.qantas.com/
Qatar Airways	866-728-2748	http://www.qatarairways.com/

R

Airline Information	Reservations Number	Website
Royal Air Maroc	800-344-6726	http://www.royalairmaroc.com/
Royal Aruban Airlines	888-2FLY-RAA	http://www.royalarubanairlines.com
Royal Jordanian Airlines	800-223-0470	http://www.rja.com.jo/
Ryan International	800-727-0457	http://www.flyryan.com/

S

Airline Information	Reservations Number	Website
Salmon Air	800-448-3413	http://www.salmonair.com/
SAS	800-221-2350	http://www.scandinavian.net/

Airline Information	Reservations Number	Website
Saudi Arabian Airlines	800-472-8342	http://www.saudiairlines.com/
Scenic Airlines	800-634-6801	http://www.scenic.com/
Seaborne Airlines	888-359-8687	http://www.seaborneairlines.com/
Singapore Airlines	800-742-3333	http://www.singaporeair.com/
South African Airways	800-722-9675	http://www.flysaa.com/
Southeast Airlines	800-359-7325	http://www.flyseal.com/
Southern Winds	800-379-9179	http://www.sw.com.ar/
Southwest Airlines	800-435-9792	http://www.southwest.com/
Spanair	888-545-5757	http://www.spanair.com/
Spirit Airlines	800-772-7117	http://www.spiritair.com/
Sri Lankan Airlines	877-915-2652	http://www.srilankan.lk/
Sun Country Airlines	800-359-6786	http://www.suncountry.com/
Surinam Airways	800-327-6864	http://www.slm.firm.sr/nl/
Swiss International Air Lines	877-359-7947	http://www.swiss.com/

T

Airline Information	Reservations Number	Website
Taca International Airlines	800-400-TACA	http://www.taca.com
Tango (Air Canada)	800-315-1390	http://www.flytango.com/
TAP Portugal	800-221-7370	http://www.flytap.com/
Taquan Air	800-770-8800	http://www.taquanair.com/
Thai Airways International	800-426-5204	http://www.thaiairways.com/
Transaero	800-957-2658	http://eagle.transaero.ru/english/
Trans North Aviation	800-451-6442	http://www.transnorth.com/
Tropic Air	800-422-3435	http://www.tropicair.com/
Turkish Airlines	800 874-8875	http://www.turkishairlines.com/

Appendix 1

U

Airline Information	Reservations Number	Website
Ukraine International Airlines	800-876-0114	http://www.ukraine-international.com/
United Airlines	800-864-8331	http://www.united.com/
US Airways	800-428-4322	http://www.usairways.com/
USA 3000 Airlines	877-872-3000	http://www.usa3000airlines.com/

V

Airline Information	Reservations Number	Website
Varig	800-468-2744	http://www.varig.com/
VASP	866-776-3869	http://www.vasp.com.br/
Virgin Atlantic Airways	800-862-8621	http://www.virgin-atlantic.com/

W

Airline Information	Reservations Number	Website
Warbelows Air Ventures	800-478-0812	http://www.warbelows.com/
Ward Air	800-478-9150	http://www.wardair.com/
West Coast Air	800-347-2222	http://www.westcoastair.com/
West Isle Airlines	800-874-4434	http://www.westisleair.com/
West Jet	800-538-5696	http://www.westjet.com/
World Airways	800-967-5310	http://www.worldair.com/
Wright Air Service	800-255-0502	http://www.wrightair.net/

Z

Airline Information	Reservations Number	Website
Zoom Airlines	866-359-9666	http://www.flyzoom.com/

If you find any airline is missing, e-mail me the information on annagooz@yahoo.com. I will add it in the next edition.

Appendix 2: Travel Arrangement Checklist

- ✓ Airline reservations

- ✓ Car rental

- ✓ Hotel reservations

- ✓ Passport for International travel - check the expiration date two months before your trip

- ✓ Visas (if needed) for International travel

- ✓ Vaccinations for International travel

- ✓ Travel insurance to cover the duration of your trip

- ✓ Get foreign currency

- ✓ Arrange for someone to take care of your home, lawn, pets, or other items as needed

- ✓ Packing

- ✓ Before leaving

    - Hold mail – this can be done online at http://www.usps.com

    - Stop newspaper delivery

    - Turn-off all unnecessary appliances

    - Turn down thermostat

- Leave emergency contact information with family or friends

- Leave unnecessary documents and keys at home

Appendix 3: Packing Checklist

Carry-on

- ✓ Money or foreign currency (cash, traveler's checks, credit cards)

- ✓ Driver's license, registration, insurance cards

- ✓ Travel documents (airline tickets, itinerary, etc.)

- ✓ Passport and visa for international travel

- ✓ Medical documents like prescriptions, vaccinations, etc.

- ✓ Birth certificate or school identifications for children

- ✓ Prescription medications – only the ones that you need during traveling

- ✓ One set of clothes for yourself

- ✓ Infant items (see infant packing check list)

- ✓ Travel pack of moisturizer, disinfecting gel, hand soap, etc.

Check-in

- ✓ Documents – keep a copy of travel itinerary, passport, prescriptions & important documents as a back up

- ✓ Prescription medications, first aid kit including painkillers, thermometer, vitamin supplements, cold and allergy medication, band-aid, and others as needed)

- ✓ Clothes

    - shirts, blouses, pants, dresses, shorts

    - underwear, socks, night dress

    - Slippers, shoes, boots

    - Accessories: belts, purses, jewelry

    - Special Occasion dress (if needed)

- ✓ Toiletries

    - Comb/brush, shampoo, conditioner, hair accessories

    - Deodorant, perfume, moisturizer, and cosmetics

    - Toothbrush, toothpaste, floss

    - Shaving needs and grooming items like nail clippers/file

    - Sanitary napkins or tampons

- ✓ Electronics you may want to carry

    - Still/video camera with batteries or charger

    - Cell phone with charger

- Laptop with charger
- CD/DVD player

✓ Glasses, sunglasses, contact lenses, cleaning solutions

✓ Optional items depending on your destination
- Umbrella
- Sun block
- Summer vacation gear: Swimming suit, sun block, hats
- Winter vacation gear: Gloves, caps, mittens, coats, sweaters
- Infant items as included in Infant's packing list

Infant's Packing Checklist

Infant's Carry-On

✓ 2 outfits for infant

✓ Diapers

✓ Wet wipes

✓ Disposable bibs

✓ Disposable changing pads (these can also be used as burp cloths)

- ✓ Large blanket that can also be used as breastfeeding cover

- ✓ Pacifier (if your infant uses them)

- ✓ Toys like rattles with gentle sounds and/or books

- ✓ Prepared formula to last the trip – take some powdered formula as backup

- ✓ Pre-packaged food jars as these do not spoil or other age appropriate snacks

- ✓ Plastic bags to dispose dirty diapers or store dirty toys/clothes

- ✓ Infant car seat or convertible car seat

- ✓ Umbrella stroller

- ✓ 2-3 sets of clothes

Infant's Suitcase

- ✓ Diapers

- ✓ Wet Wipes

- ✓ Clothes

- ✓ Socks and shoes

- ✓ Cloth bibs

- ✓ Infant toiletries: toothbrush, toothpaste, soap, etc

- ✓ Medications, if any
- ✓ 2-3 bottles, bottle brush, sippy cup (if needed)
- ✓ Infant formula and food (enough to give you time to find a place to buy some at your destination)
- ✓ Portable playpen: This can also be used as crib. This is an optional item and will have to checked-in as a separate baggage item.
- ✓ Toys, books, and other items for entertaining the infant
- ✓ Optional items
    - Infant proofing items
    - Night light
    - Infant monitor
    - Infant carrie

Appendix 4: Consent Letter

To Whom It May Concern

I, _____ (full name of the parent/legal guardian) of _____ (address), am the _____ (parent/legal guardian) of:

Child's full name: _____

Date of birth: _____

Place of birth: _____

Passport number: _____

_____ (child's full name), has my consent to travel with _____ (Full name of accompanying parent) of _____ (address of the accompanying parent) to visit _____ (name of foreign country) during the period of _____ (dates of travel: departure and return). During that period, _____ (child's full name) will be residing with _____ (name of accompanying parent) at _____ _____ (address where child will be residing in foreign country).

Any questions regarding this consent letter can be directed to the undersigned.

Signature:_____
Date:_____

(Full name and signature of the parent)

Signed before me, _____ (name of witness), this _____ (date) at _____ _____ (name of location).

Signature: _____ (name of witness)

Appendix 4

You should carry a consent letter from the other parent, if you are traveling alone with the children. This sample consent letter can be amended to meet your specific needs.

Appendix 5: List of Prohibited Items

Here is the modified list of prohibited objects from the TSA website as of March 2010. Check the website at http://www.tsa.gov/travelers/airtravel/prohibited/permitted-prohibited-items.shtm for the latest list.

Sharp Objects

Item	Carry-on	Checked
Box Cutters	No	Yes
Knives - except for plastic knives	No	Yes
Razor-blades (box cutter type)	No	Yes
Scissors	Yes	Yes
Swords/sabers	No	Yes

Sporting Goods

Item	Carry-on	Checked
Baseball Bats	No	Yes
Bows and Arrows	No	Yes
Cricket Bats	No	Yes
Golf Clubs	No	Yes
Hockey Sticks	No	Yes
Lacrosse Sticks	No	Yes
Pool Cues	No	Yes
Ski Poles	No	Yes

Guns & Firearms

Item	Carry-on	Checked
Ammunition – must be declared if being carried in checked bag.	No	Yes
BB guns/Pellet Guns	No	Yes
Firearms - firearms carried as checked baggage MUST be unloaded.	No	Yes
NOTE: Check with your airline to see if firearms are allowed in the checked baggage and rules that apply.		

Tools

Item	Carry-on	Checked
Axes, Hatchets, Saw	No	Yes
Hammers	No	Yes
Drills and drill bits (including cordless portable power drills)	No	Yes
Screwdrivers, wrenches, pliers (small one are allowed on carry-on)	No	Yes

Other Items

Item	Carry-on	Checked
Candles	No	Yes
Gel shoe inserts	No	Yes
Snow globes like decorations that contain water	No	Yes

Resources

American Academy of Pediatrics: policy statement and recommendations, http://www.aap.org/family/cps.htm

Center for Disease Control and Prevention: Resources for traveling with children http://www.cdc.gov/travel/child_travel.htm

Federal Aviation Administration: Flying with Children, http://www.faa.gov/passengers/fly_children/

TSA: Travel with children http://www.tsa.gov/travelers/airtravel/children/index.shtm

US Department of State: Documentation requirements, http://travel.state.gov/travel/cbpmc/cbpmc_2223.html

Airline Website Consulted:

American Airlines, http://www.aa.com

Southwest, http://www.southwest.com

Air Canada, http://www.aircanada.com

Other Website Consulted:

About.com: Air travel guides and tips http://airtravel.about.com/

About.com: Baby products,
http://babyproducts.about.com/od/travel/bb/babyairtravel.htm

Air Safe: Critical information for traveling public,
http://www.airsafe.com/kidsafe/kidrules.htm

Cyber parent,
http://www.cyberparent.com/trips/fly.htm

Family fun: Advice and ideas about vacationing with children, http://familyfun.go.com/vacations/

Flying with Kids: website with practical travel advice and travel accessories,
http://www.flyingwithkids.com/

Moms-in-minivan,
http://www.momsminivan.com/article-flying_with_children.html

www.ingramcontent.com/pod-product-compliance
Lightning Source LLC
LaVergne TN
LVHW051601070426
835507LV00021B/2701